This Book Belongs To:

_____

CORNERSTONE

A MOMENTS WITH

JESUS

ENCOUNTER BIBLE

20 Immersive Accounts of Jesus from Throughout the Scriptures

DESTINY IMAGE® PUBLISHERS, INC.
PO Box 310, Shippensburg, PA 17257-0310

"Publishing cutting-edge prophetic resources to supernaturally empower the body of Christ"

This book and all other Destiny Image and Destiny Image Fiction books are available at Christian bookstores and distributors worldwide.

Illustrations by Kevin and Kristen Howdeshell

For more information on foreign distributors, call 717-532-3040.

Or reach us on the Internet: www.destinyimage.com

ISBN 13 TP: 978-0-7684-6302-6

ISBN 13 EBook: 978-0-7684-6303-3

For Worldwide Distribution

Printed by Thomson Press (I) Ltd., Faridabad, Haryana, India

1 2 3 4 5 6 / 27 26 25 24

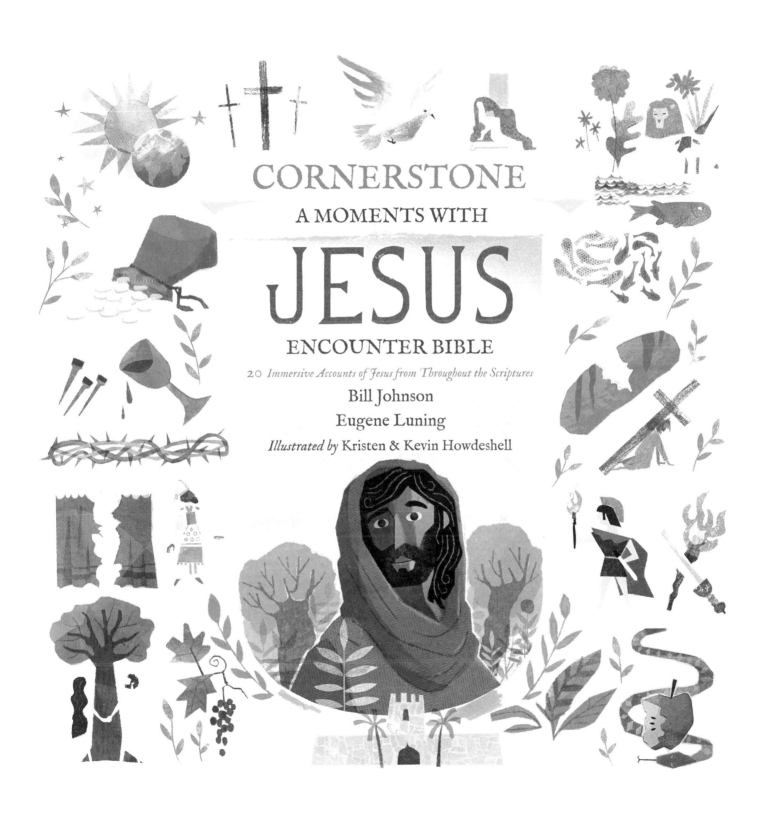

CORNERSTONE

A MOMENTS WITH

JESUS

ENCOUNTER BIBLE

20 Immersive Accounts of Jesus from Throughout the Scriptures

Bill Johnson

Eugene Luning

Illustrated by Kristen & Kevin Howdeshell

Acknowledgements

Kevin & Kristen Howdeshell

Thank you to Christian and Eugene for trusting us with the illustrations and for giving us much creative freedom.

Contents

Introduction
by Bill Johnson

Our greatest priority is to focus ourselves and our families on the presence of God. As parents and guardians, we are the culture-makers of our home. We are the ones who set the atmosphere. It is our privilege to model intimacy with the Lord, revealing our values through our actions. Entrusted with these precious lives, our main goal is to help children foster their own relationship with God and their own intimacy with the Holy Spirit. There is no junior Holy Spirit. Children do not receive a miniature version of God. In fact, Jesus tells us to model ourselves after the curiosity, wonder, and open-hearted trust that children exemplify. Young people are meant to have a vibrant, powerful, authentic relationship with God. And we can help develop that.

When Beni and I were raising our kids, we prioritized living out our relationship with God in front of them. They were with us when we were praying, worshipping, or reading the Bible. They listened to us repent for bad attitudes and repair relationships. They grew up knowing that hearing from God was natural and easy. We were intentional about building culture, not only at Bethel, but also in our home. Over many years, we have distilled that culture down to four pillars of belief. These four cornerstones of our faith undergird everything that we do. They are the values that form the foundation of our teaching, our programming, and our vision. My prayer is that they can be a guide to your family as you bring up the next generation of powerful believers.

God Is Good. He is so much better than we think. It is our job, then, to change the way we think. God is consistently good. He doesn't fluctuate between being a loving Father and an abusive one. Our Father God is so kind, so wonderfully encouraging, and so perfectly strengthening. He sees the brokenness of the world and wants to change that—no question. But He is a patient, loving God who works in and through His people to bring about those changes.

Our beliefs must impact our behaviors. So, if we believe that God is good, we must dream big. In Scripture, He promises that He is able to do *"above all that we ask or think"* (Ephesians 3:20). That means His goodness is beyond the reach of our prayer life—our asking—and beyond the reach of our imagination— our thinking. That's His covenant with us. When we truly know that, we begin to dream about what might be possible in our lifetime. What could we see happen in and through our family? What could our children see take place in their schools? God wants to do more in them, through them, and for them than they ever thought was possible.

Everyone Is Significant. God doesn't make junk. And yet, tragically, so many people—adults and children—don't know how significant they are in God's eyes. He has poured Himself out on us because of the value He sees in every single person. The value of something is always determined by how much someone is willing to pay for it, and Jesus paid the ultimate price for each one of us. That significance must be realized. It's not a significance that leads to arrogance, but rather to gratitude, celebration, and a desire to give God our all.

In John 13, Jesus and the disciples had just finished eating dinner. Verses 3-4 say, *"Jesus, knowing that the Father had given all things into His hands, and that He had come from God and was going to God, rose from supper and laid aside His garments, took a towel and girded Himself"*

(NKJV). Jesus, understanding His significance and authority, picked up a towel and washed the disciples' feet. The result of knowing His value was humble service to others. When we truly understand how precious we are, we also know that every person is worthy of honor, celebration, and respect because we know the One who intentionally created them.

Jesus' Blood Paid for Everything. Everything was purchased at Calvary. Ephesians 2:7 says that *"in the ages to come He might show the exceeding riches of His grace in His kindness toward us in Christ Jesus"* (NKJV). We know that we are saved by grace, the favor of God that was given to us through the blood of Jesus. This verse shows us that we will continue to learn about that grace throughout eternity. On the cross, Jesus purchased everything we would need both in this lifetime—every healing, every victory over darkness, every resurrection over death—but also throughout eternity. One hundred billion years from now, we will still not have discovered all that was purchased at Calvary.

Because His blood has gone before us and paid for everything we will ever need, He deserves our unreserved trust. It is healthy for our children to see that when disappointment happens or circumstances turn out differently than what we prayed for, we still hold onto the truth of the cross. Yes, we've been forgiven for our sins. Yes, His blood washes us clean and makes us acceptable before the Father. But, the cross also reveals the fact that Jesus took upon Himself all that I deserved so that I could receive all that He deserved. That is astounding. That is the power of the blood.

Nothing Is Impossible. It would seem obvious that nothing is impossible for God. He is the Lord, the omnipotent Creator of the universe. But His Word also says that "with God nothing is impossible" (see Luke 1:37). We are the ones who are with God. His Kingdom is a realm where nothing is impossible, but He wanted those made in His image to know what that realm is like. He gave us access to that realm through our faith in Him. The great privilege of the believer is to consider that there is nothing outside of the reach of His goodness or power. We have been given the privilege to invade the realm called "impossible."

Because we have been given this access, we must be willing to take risks. We must teach our children to look for opportunities for God to invade situations that feel impossible. We must model allowing ourselves to be inconvenienced to see His Kingdom come. As you read through the stories in the following pages, you will see Jesus invading the impossible day after day. He looked for opportunities to bring heaven to earth. And then He said that we would do *"greater works than these"* (John 14:12). Meditating on this reality will drive us toward taking risks so that Jesus will be seen for who He is on the earth.

These four pillars of belief have been the foundation for how we do life. They have helped guide our thinking and behavior as we've built our lives around the chief cornerstone: Jesus Christ. He is our anchor, our hope, and the center of our lives. As you read through these beautifully imagined stories from the Bible, let yourself be drawn toward Him. My prayer is that these stories bring to life the truth of the Scriptures for both you and your children. May it ignite a fire in your family for more of Him. May we raise a generation of children who stand securely on their knowledge of who God is and who He has created them to be: an unstoppable force for His Kingdom.

Bill Johnson,
Bethel Church, Redding, CA

Part I

God Is Good

Chapter 1

The Word Who Created Everything

Imagine seeing nothing, hearing nothing, smelling nothing, tasting nothing, touching nothing, because—

there is nothing.

In place of the planet Earth, the moon above, the planets, sun, stars, galaxies, the universe—

there's nothing at all.

Instead of mountains, oceans, sunsets, rivers, hills, deserts, streams, forests, snowy arctics—

a total blank space.

Rather than red, orange, yellow, green, blue, indigo, and violet sparkling with wonder—

utter darkness.

And then imagine...

...this!

Well,
here's the story...

Before anything was, God was. He was Himself before there was anything else at all. There was no beginning—there can be no end—to God. He is the first and the last, the start and finish. He is both the Pioneer and the Perfecter of all things.

He is the sight, the sound, the smell, the taste, the feel of what it means to *be*. He is how we know the things we know. He is the place we may live, the beauty of all we'll experience, the wonder beyond our wildest dreams. His is the loveliest sort of love. He is the highest heights, the furthest distances, the most colorful of colors, the ultimate of experiences. He is everything our heart desires. His is the love, the warmth, the brightness, the newness, the freshness, the royal splendor, the awesome wonder of all that fills us with gladness, with joy!

God is so good!

Just imagine what He might do next!

And so then came **The Beginning**—from the heart of the God who was there *before* the beginning of the beginning. ***It's time now***, He decided—and with that He began time...

And there was something about God so bright and beautiful, so sparkling and glorious that He had to make sure you and I would see it. So He said with His Word, "Let there be light!"

And all at once, there it was: LIGHT!

It was bright and beautiful, sparkling and glorious—*so good!*

Because God is good.

And there was something about God so high and heavenly, so mysterious and wonderful that He had to make sure you and I would see it. So He said with His Word, "Let there be heavens!"

And all at once there they were: THE HEAVENS!

They were high and heavenly, mysterious and wonderful—*so good!*

Because God is good.

And there was something about God so interesting and deep, so unexpected and gorgeous that He had to make sure you and I would see it. So He said with His Word, "Let there be earth and seas!"

And all at once there they were: THE EARTH AND THE SEAS!

They were interesting and deep, unexpected and gorgeous—*so good!*

Because God is good.

And there was something about God so colorful and rich, so spectacular and breathtaking that He had to make sure you and I would see it. So He said with His Word, "Let there be plants and trees and flowers!"

And all at once there they were: PLANTS AND TREES AND FLOWERS!

They were colorful and rich, spectacular and breathtaking—
so good!

Because God is good.

And there was something about God so life-giving and warm, so haunting, so jaw-dropping that He had to make sure you and I would see it. So He said with His Word, "Let there be sun and moon and stars!"

And all at once there they were: THE SUN AND MOON AND STARS!

They were life-giving and warm, haunting and jaw-dropping—*so good!*

Because God is good.

And there was something about God so unending and perfectly lovely, so hilarious and fascinating that He had to make sure you and I would see it. So He said with His Word, "Let there be every creature under the sun!"

And all at once there they were: ALL GOD'S CREATURES!

They were unending and perfectly lovely, hilarious and fascinating—*so good!*

Because God is good.

And there was still more to come...

Just you wait!

Imagine opening up your eyes—blinking your
eyelids, squinting against the light, letting your sight
adjust—*as the very first person God made!*

You are looking around at the beauties of a beautiful garden,
in the fresh morning sunlight, and you are seeing everything He made
before He made you:

All the wondrous brightness, the heavens overhead, the earth beneath your feet,
the streams, lakes, rivers, and oceans sparkling with a million-billion points of light...

The perfections of the colorful flowers, plants, and trees, all lit up by the sun...

The sights and sounds, the colors and cackles of a thousand-thousand
glorious, wonderful animals...

You stand up to your feet. (This is your first time ever walking!) You begin to walk around the garden and *look*, *listen*, *smell*, *taste,* and *touch* all the glorious things that God has made.

You feel the way your heart is leaping—you are absolutely overwhelmed!

You can hardly handle the loveliness of His goodness!

And then, suddenly, you turn and see *Him*—

The One who made it all—

He is standing in the garden watching you!

He calls you to come nearer. He wants you standing by His side under the shade of the trees. "I am the Word of Life," He says. "I made you. I love you. Now let's walk the garden in this coolness of the new day."

Let's Talk about It

What is your favorite part of creation? What does that part of creation show you about who God is?

Imagine that you are walking with God in the garden like Adam did. What kinds of things do you think God would say to you?

Chapter 2

The Knowledge
of Evil and Good

Imagine a man and woman—the first man and woman—taking a walk through the garden in the stillness of the evening. They follow a winding trail through its beautiful tall trees, listening to the sound of the breeze through the leaves and branches. The edges of the trail are thick with colorful wildflowers. The colors of sunset make everything feel peaceful.

They arrive at a clearing; up ahead they see a meadow. Amidst the tall grasses they can see the strolling, running, leaping, and hopping of more kinds of animals than you can possibly imagine. They see herds of cows, flocks of sheep, prides of lions, caravans of camels, parades of elephants, troops of kangaroos, streaks of tigers, stands of flamingos, and, overhead, what look like bright clouds of all the flapping birds of the air. Everywhere they look they see the glories of all God made for them.

They continue along, walking.

As they cross the open meadow, they are walking toward the crystal-clear waters of the great river of the Garden of Eden. It flows along in lovely, powerful silence; in the distance, they can hear the place its waters tumble down through the large rocks. Beyond the river, the foothills rise and roll upward; behind the foothills climb the huge, mighty mountains of Eden's outer range. The sunset light is dimming down upon everything—the mountains, waters, animals, and trees are settling down for the night. The air around them is getting cooler too.

The man and woman are nearly where they're going.

Past the clearing and following the bank of the river—the evening getting quite dark around them now—they walk toward the *true* center of the garden. Everything around them—all the trees, grasses, animals, foothills, mountains, skies above—seem to lean toward this place. This place holds two trees, planted there by God: the tree of life and the tree of the knowledge of good and evil. The two trees stand there in the middle of the garden, full of bright, rich-looking fruit, and yet these trees are very different.

The tree of life bears fruit that *gives* everlasting life.

The fruit of the other tree will *steal, kill,* and *destroy* life.

The man and woman arrive at the place between these two great trees. In the darkness, they lie down to sleep.

The woman, Eve, awakes to the sound of a voice: *"Eve!"* All around her is darkness. She hears the hissing of this dark, evil, angry-sounding voice and sees it belongs to a dark, slithering snake.

"Eve," the snake whispers again, hissing out her name. "Come with me over here, will you?"

Eve rises to her feet. She follows the snake toward one of the two great trees—the forbidden tree of the knowledge of good and evil. The snake's eyes open wide in the moonlight. He gestures with his head toward the great tree.

"Did God *really* say that you can't have *any* fruit from *any* tree in the garden?" he asked her.

"No," Eve answered. "That's not what God said. He said we could eat the fruit of *any* tree in the whole of the garden; we just can't eat the fruit from *this* one. We're not even supposed to touch it. God said that this tree and its fruit will lead to death."

The dark snake laughed into the dark night. "How silly!" he hissed. "You won't die if you eat of this fruit. In fact, eating this fruit will open your eyes and heart to knowing both good *and* evil. You will become *like* God. That's the reason He doesn't want you to eat it. You see, He's not as good as you think He is."

Eve listened closely to this lie. She began looking at the beautiful tall tree with its beautiful fruit, and she watched the way the moonlight lit its beautiful leaves. She began to want to try its fruit for herself. She began to want to be like God—*to be God*.

Reaching out, she picked a piece of its fruit, took a bite, swallowed it down—and suddenly felt very alone. The snake had disappeared—but it wasn't him Eve missed. It was something inside herself that suddenly felt broken.

She woke her husband and talked to him of her loneliness and asked if he might like to try some of the same fruit. Her husband, Adam, joined with her in disobeying God's command. And he too suddenly felt all alone.

In the morning, they decided to go back to where they'd come from; they started walking, their journey across the garden. They left behind the two great trees—the garden's true center—and headed toward that nearest bank of the river. The far eastern mountains were hidden behind dark, terrible clouds; there was wind and hail and furious storms lashing their summits. The foothills had a worn, old look, like they hadn't seen rain in many ages. The sunlight on the waters of the river looked strangely harsh; they tried to hide their eyes from its glaring reflection.

And when they reached the clearing, the great meadow...

What they saw there broke their hearts...

In place of yesterday's peace and quiet—all the joyous strolling, running, leaping, and hopping—all the animals seemed to be at war. The cows and sheep were running from the lions; the camels and flamingos were hiding from the tigers. It was like everything, all at once, had gone so terribly wrong.

They hurried through the meadow and followed along the pathway through the trees. But everything here seemed different too. All the wildflowers were wilting, losing their colors. The trees of the forest seemed sad and lifeless.

Adam and Eve looked at each other and their hearts broke.

And then they heard the footsteps of the Word.

"My children," the Word said, "where are you? Where have you gone?"

Adam and Eve didn't know what to say—so they stayed quiet.

"Adam and Eve, My children!" the Word said more loudly, yet with love. "Come! I want to go on one of our walks!"

Adam and Eve stepped out from their hiding spot and faced the Word. He looked at them, puzzled. "Why do you have that look in your eyes?" He asked.

"Because," Adam replied, "we feel ashamed, afraid."

The eyes of the Word grew narrow. "Who told you about shame and fear?" He asked them. "Did you eat from the tree of the knowledge of good and evil?"

Adam and Eve looked down at the ground. They tried to make excuses for their actions. They didn't know what to do or say.

Yet when they looked up into the eyes of the One who'd created them, delighted in them, they simply saw that He was heartbroken. Great glorious tears were running down His cheeks as He regarded Eve and Adam with sadness—and with love.

They had broken the heart of God into pieces.

And yet His love was bigger than anything they might do.

The Word walked them sadly toward the farthest edge of the garden, told them they must go, and yet told them something else too:

"My daughter, My son," He said to them, holding them by the hand, *"you have broken our first fellowship. My goodness will be a mystery to you for a time, but not forever. I will show My face to your children's children. I will make this broken way new again. I will return for all people. I will make right the damage done. I will destroy the power of the evil one. I promise.*

"I promise upon Myself."

Let's Talk about It

Have you ever done something you know you weren't supposed to do? How did that make you feel?

Why do you think God's heart was broken by what Adam and Eve did?

What do you think it felt like to be so loved even after they'd done something wrong? Has that ever happened to you?

Chapter 3

A King Sees the King

Imagine, many years later, a king in the library of his castle. He is sitting upon a beautiful golden chair, robed in a silky long cloak; his feet are comfortably set in rich kingly slippers. He has just taken off his crown and set it upon his desk. The morning sunlight is coming in through the open window. He is sitting in this library—this place he likes to speak of as his "study"—studying the words that are written on an ancient scroll. The scroll is wound out to where he's reading to himself these words:

When Eve saw that the tree was good for food, and that it was beautiful to the eyes, and that the tree could also make her wise, she took some of its fruit, and ate it. Then she gave some to her husband, Adam, and he had some, too. Then both their eyes were opened, and suddenly they knew that they hadn't been wearing any clothes. So they sewed some fig leaves together and made coverings for themselves. And they heard God's voice walking in the garden in the cool of the day, and the man and his wife hid themselves from the presence of God among the trees of the garden.

God called to Adam and Eve, and said to them, "Where are you?"[1]

King David sighs a sigh of sadness. He rises up from that golden chair in his study, crosses across the room, down the hall, down some stairs, and out into his gardens. The day outside is a fresh, beautiful day. He strolls amidst the flowers, trees, vines, the sculpted bushes, the long pools of water, talking aloud to God. He prays, from a sad heart, in these words:

1   Genesis 3:6–9 paraphrased.

I'm afraid I don't love you the way I should, God.

I'm so full of myself, so full of myself that I crowd you out.

Sometimes I lie and stretch the truth as far as it can go.

Oftentimes, I'm too busy to listen to you and to learn.

I forget to do the right thing almost all the time.

When I wake,
it's as if doing the wrong thing is my first thought.

I follow so many ways that are not good at all.

I forget to run away from doing wrong.

Oh God! I'm so sad to be so broken![2]

King David is making his way to the farthest corner of his garden. There, he enters through a door that takes him up a spiraling staircase—up, up, up—until he arrives at the top of a stone tower. The outside top of the tower looks down over the city. He begins to watch his people going about the course of their day. He sees people shouting at each other in the marketplace, mothers and fathers and children getting into sad, silly arguments, a fight breaking out in the nearby schoolyard. He hears the sounds of anger, the laughter of cruel mockery, loud cursing, a little child crying all by herself.

2   An adaptation of Psalm 36.

King David raises his hands over his city and begins praying again:

Oh! how sad it makes my heart, my spirit, Lord God!

The hatefulness of our ways is too much for us.

Our anger shoots out to hurt all those around us.

We do the wrong thing when we mean to do the right;

We are so confused in our hearts and minds.

Please don't leave us broken, O Lord God!

O Lord God, please come nearer, nearer!

Please hurry here to help us!

O Lord God, only you can save us![3]

King David opens his eyes...

And something unexpected is happening...

As the eyes of his heart are suddenly open to God.

King David is seeing...

---

3   An adaptation of Psalm 38.

47

A vision!

He is seeing what is to come:

A Man—a smiling, joyous, bearded Man—a Man whose face is lit with love and hope and laughter;

A Man who carries the Way of God, the Law of God, within His heart, who is perfect and can make us perfect;

A Man who gives His life so sin, death, sadness, brokenness, sorrow are all ended— forever and ever;

A Man whom death cannot kill—who, giving away His life, will end all fear of death for everyone.

As he looks, King David hears a voice from Heaven. It booms aloud in his ears:

> *"I have heard your prayers. And behold! I will send a Rescuer. They will call this Man the Son of Man, the Son of David, the Son of God. He will sit upon your throne forever. He will come to be the Savior of all."*

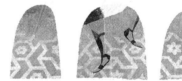

There are now tears running down the face of King David. Happy tears of laughter. Tears of joy and of fresh new life.

King David is overjoyed.

And once again he raises his hands over the city, over the whole world, and begins to shout aloud his praise:

My heart is happy and my mouth rejoices;

Every part of me is at peace now,

*Because you never leave us alone,
never leave us in fear,*

*We will never see the darkness
of death.*

You yourself are the Way of life;

Your presence with us is joy;

At your right hand is all good pleasure.[4]

You will lift us up to Heaven, O God!

You will rescue all your people!

Even the worst of the worst!

You desire to live within us!

Thank you, my God and my Savior!

Every single day, you carry me!

You are the God who will save us!

You are the God who saves our souls from death![5]

The people in the streets of Jerusalem can hear the shouts of King David, echoing across the rooftops, dancing along the cobbles, landing within their hearts and minds.

"God, You are so, so good!" King David shouts over the city. *"So, so good!"*

And his people, looking up at him, begin to believe.

---

4   An adaptation of Psalm 16.
5   An adaptation of Psalm 68.

Let's Talk about It

If you were totally honest with God about how you feel right now, what would that sound like?

Why do you think King David was so happy after he saw the vision? What do you think he was feeling?

Chapter 4

A Great Test

Imagine, many years later, an enormous crowd on the banks of a river. They are spread across the golden-brown hills, rising and falling with the ups and downs, right up to the edges of the flowing waters. The river's water sails by, greenish-gray. The colors of the sunset are beautiful through the branches of the trees. These men, women, and children are still and silent, facing in the direction of the river.

You see, just moments ago, a Man went wading out past the others in the water. He approached John the Baptist; the two of them spoke to each other quietly. Then John the Baptist laid the Man against his arms, dunked Him down in the water, and, like everyone else, raised Him up with a fast, splashing lift.

Suddenly something unbelievable was happening...

As the sunset sky overhead seemed to be tearing apart...

And out of that heavenly tearing, a dove was winging its way down...

And seemed to settle upon the Man in the water with John the Baptist.

Then, with a rumbling sound—like the meeting of an earthquake and the long roll of summer thunder—came a voice speaking aloud from the heavens. *"You are My dearly loved Son!"* the voice said to the Man. *"I am so very pleased with You!"*

Everyone in the riverbanks crowd was terribly frightened. Fathers and mothers gathered their children close. All the children tried to act brave for each other. No one knew what to think. And even as they stood there shaking at this strange thing they'd all witnessed, they missed seeing something else happening.

That Man was passing along, right by them—through the crowds, under the shadows of the low trees, and off toward the wilderness. He too had heard that voice of His Father—and another, that of the Holy Spirit—and it was time for Him to go.

Night fell on that Man, Jesus, walking. He was hiking away from the river valley. He was following the voice of the Spirit, past the places of people, cities, towns, houses, comfort, walking in obedience. He continued into the dry, silent, rocky, craggy places of the desert, listening to the sounds of the wild animals calling. The moon rose and lit the reddish faces of the hills; He found a place to sit down, to rest.

"Well, Father," He said as He was falling asleep that night, "I have come here to be with You alone."

The next morning and for the forty mornings, noondays, afternoons, and evenings to follow, Jesus did exactly the same thing: He woke up with the sun, took a drink of water from a spring nearby, and then talked to and listened to His heavenly Father. That was all He did for the next forty days. The sun would rise and climb and crest and fall and set behind the hills: Jesus would only be with His heavenly Father. The western wind would whisper and whip; the desert sands would swirl and whirl. All Jesus noticed was the voice of the Spirit of God.

And for all those forty days, He ate nothing. He needed nothing. The presence of His Father was His food, His strength.

Yet at the end of those forty days, Jesus was tired. He was sunburnt. He was hungry. And that was when it began.

A dark figure approached from the shadows. He seemed to come out of nowhere. This evil figure suddenly was standing at the side of Jesus. He watched Jesus, looking at the side of His face, thinking. Then, with a dark, evil, angry-sounding, hissing voice, he spoke these words: "If You really are the Son of God, make all these stones bread. Go ahead. Make Yourself something to eat."

Jesus didn't even turn to look at this dark one. With a quiet, steady voice, He answered him, simply, "Man doesn't live only on bread. It is the scriptures that have told us that. Man is meant to live by listening to the words of God."

The dark figure grunted. Groaned. He was angry at the steadiness of Jesus. Then he snapped his fingers and—*just like that!*—the two of them were standing upon a high mountain, looking out over the rooftops of the world. All around them were the people of the earth, the kingdoms of men, the palaces, fortresses, treasure vaults; and the evil one said to Jesus, "I can give You all of this. All of these earthly things are things within my power. Just fall down and worship me—give me some of Your heart—and I'll give You all the finest things in the world."

Jesus sighed to Himself. He looked at all those people down below, waiting on a Savior. Then He said with a voice growing louder, ever more steady, "I will worship the Lord God and serve Him only. For that is what the scriptures say to do."

Again, the dark one at his side groaned. He let out a sound that was almost like pain. Then he snapped his fingers and—*Just like that!*—the two of them were in Jerusalem, the capital city, and they were standing upon a high tower. Behind them were the worship places of the Temple; before them, a garden called Gethsemane.

"If You really are the Son of God," he growled to Jesus, pointing down, "go ahead, *jump!* For don't the scriptures say, 'God will send angels to help You and guard You, and they will keep You safe'?"

Jesus turned and looked directly into the darkness of that face. He was powerful in the presence of this evil. And He held forth His fist as He spoke aloud these words, "You shall not test God!"

And all at once they were back in the wilderness. They were back to the exact place they started. The darkness of the evil one was dimming, just like a sunset fades. He had tried out all his tests upon Jesus—and he knew he was defeated by the presence of this Man.

Into the darkness the devil slinked away...

And the goodness, the righteousness of God, won this first battle.

The Rescuer had come.

Let's Talk about It

How do you think Jesus was feeling after His forty-day fast?

Why do you think the devil wanted Jesus to worship him? Have you ever had an experience where you felt tempted to do something, but you resisted?

Chapter 5

The Beginning of the Beginning

Imagine standing next to John the Baptist near the River Jordan. It is early morning; the air is cool and somewhat misty. That scent in the air is the scent of the river, the trees, the flowers, the dusty dirt. The sun is starting to climb over the far eastern distances. The shadows around you are especially long. John and you and another friend are having a morning chat. The daytime crowds haven't yet arrived from Jerusalem.

You are about to say something to John the Baptist and your friend when...

John's eyes open wide.

He leans to the side to look past you, beyond you. He is looking up a narrow trail, descending. His eyes sparkle with a sudden sense of heavenly wonder. *"Look!"* he says, pointing up. "Here comes the Lamb of God, the Savior!"

Turning, you see that Man who, more than a month before this, came to the waters, talked with John, received John's baptism—*the One for whom the heavens tore open!* Today, He is walking down the hillside, casually. He seems to be having an altogether pleasant sort of morning.

You turn back to look at John the Baptist.

John the Baptist, smiling, was already looking at you.

"Go!" he says to you. "Follow after Him!"

As Jesus passes, whistling a little tune under His breath, He doesn't even stop to pass the time of day with John, with you, with your other friend. He simply continues on. He hits the bend of the road, just above this branch of the river, and continues walking.

You and your friend look over at each other. Both of you are considering the choice before you.

Then—in what will be the greatest moment of decision in the history of your whole life—the two of you begin to follow after Jesus. He is walking swiftly across the plain above the river. You and your friend begin to run in order to catch up.

The whole morning passes by...

Lunchtime comes...

The afternoon goes...

This whole day, you and your friend have been a few steps back from Jesus, watching Him walk, wondering when He might stop, might rest. *Has He even noticed the two of us back here?* you wonder to yourself. You simply continue on, following.

Now you are climbing up a long, back-and-forth switchback trail, trying to keep up, with the sunlight slowly starting to drop in the west; you are just putting one foot in front of the other, sweating, struggling, breathing short hard breaths, when suddenly...

He turns.

He has stopped at a bend in the narrow trail. He turns around smoothly—and grinning. His head leans off to one side, looking at the pair of you. He is considering you both. He is looking deeply into your eyes.

"So what is it you want?" Jesus asks. These are the very first words He ever says to you.

You're not quite sure how to answer Him. "Well..." you say, uncertainly, "where are You staying tonight?"

Jesus laughs. He makes a motion for you to come up and walk with Him. "Come along and see," He says.

That night, the moon is hanging nearly full and extra bright over the hills; its gray-white light makes everything seem to shine. The leaves on the trees, the roofs of the houses in this small village, everyone's cloaks and tunics—all of it has a warm, lit-up look. You are sitting across a table from Jesus in the open air. You have already finished your first supper together. It's just you and Jesus relaxing.

By the light of the rising moon, you watch Him.

You watch the peacefulness of His face closely.

He takes up His cup, drinks a long, slow sip, and puts it down. He smiles. "I am so glad you're with Me now," He says to you. "It's going to be good. *Very* good."

This is a night you are certain you will never forget.

Let's Talk about It

What would the two have had to leave behind to follow Jesus?

Imagine you're camping out with Jesus. What would you talk about? What would you laugh with Him about? What kinds of questions would you want to ask?

Part II

Each Person Is Significant

Chapter 6

The Stranger by the Pool

Imagine lying in the hottest heat next to a little pool. You are lying there upon an old straw mat. You can feel the heat of the midday upon your face and over the length of your body. It feels altogether too warm, uncomfortable. Every once in a while a breeze starts to blow and yet it doesn't do a thing to cool you down. The sky overhead is, off and on, coated over with big clouds. But the sunshine beats down on you, almost despite those clouds.

All around the pool are other people too, and around this whole tiled pool area is a series of tall mighty columns with roofs overtop them. This big open-air square is in the northern part of Jerusalem, just north of the Temple. These columns surrounding you feel almost like a prison; they feel like fences keeping you stuck inside this place.

Also, you cannot walk. The legs stretching out on your mat have no feeling, no strength, no sensation.

For a very long time you have never taken a step anywhere. You haven't been able to go for a stroll, haven't explored the woods by just walking out there, haven't been able to play the games you used to play. Instead—*for almost forty years!*—your days have been the longest sorts of days imaginable: dragging yourself around, begging for bread, hoping to meet a kind stranger who will help you.

Long ago, you heard of this place—the pool of Bethesda, just north of the Temple— and since then you have waited here by the poolside. The waters of this pool have an amazing reputation. Every once in a while, the top of the waters gets stirred by the touch of an angel; if you're the first one in, you'll be healed—*made whole again!*

Except...

The waters hardly ever seem to stir.

And when they do...

You are never the first one in.

It has been many years since you really, truly believed any good could happen to you; you long ago lost an important thing:

Hope.

This morning has been a typical morning: waking up, eating some old dry bread, starting at once to watch the pool for any sign of movement. Everyone else is waking up too: groaning, grunting, crying a little bit to themselves; these are the usual sounds of the morning here. The whole day long you are *expecting* to watch the waters, *expecting* nothing much to happen, *expecting* to fall asleep tonight disappointed.

And right about then, you see Him.

Right over there.

He is standing in the shadow cast by the tall columns.

This Man, standing surrounded by a group of other men and women, stands there in the shade, looking like He is looking for something.

Or, perhaps, for *someone*.

You see His eyes moving across the seas of sick, helpless people, and they suddenly stop upon *you*. His eyes almost move along, but then they bounce back. The Man then smiles ear to ear, His eyes light up, and He starts making His way over toward *you*. He bobs and weaves, He zigs and zags, He follows the tilework of the courtyard until, finally...

He is standing directly in front of *you.*

Then He kneels down right by your side.

And places His hand upon your shoulder.

You have almost forgotten the feeling of how that sort of touch can feel—such a feeling of warmth and kindness, such a sense of true-hearted love. And in the whole of your life, you have never seen eyes like the Man's—so full of goodness, kindness, of deep, deep affection.

"Would you like to walk?" the Man asks.

Your heart hurts at the wording of such a question. (Truth be told, you have given up any idea of ever walking again many, many years ago.) So you reply, "It's impossible, Sir. I can never get into the pool when the stirring of the waters happens."

The Man is looking directly into your eyes. His broad smile has become a joyous grin.

Then He says to you, "Pick up your mat! Walk! Let's get going!"

You look around at the other people around you—all those sick, helpless people—and you feel almost embarrassed, somewhat silly. *What a strange sort of thing to say!* you are thinking to yourself...

Then you look again into the eyes of the Man...

Eyes that have suddenly grown very serious...

And that's the moment when you suddenly realize *feeling* is starting to creep up from your feet, through your ankles, up to the backs of your knees!

That's the instant when a *strength* starts to move its way from His words into your body. *He has healed you!*

Before you know it, you are on your feet—*STANDING!*—you are moving around—*WALKING!*—you are running around the courtyard—*DANCING!*

The whole Pool of Bethesda is filled with *SHOUTS*, echoing with *CHEERS*, bubbling over with *SINGING*. The whole place is a wild scene!

Except, you realize, the Man has disappeared...

Before you could find out His name or who He is...

So you *walk* out, looking for Him.

Let's Talk about It

Have you ever wanted something for a really long time without getting it? What was that like for you?

What do you think it felt like when Jesus locked eyes with the man laying beside the pool?

Draw a picture of the man before and after encountering Jesus!

Chapter 7

A Surprising Choice

Imagine a man walking through the streets of his town. He just finished breakfast, said goodbye to his wife and children and servants; he is walking along enjoying the feeling of the morning. The sun is climbing higher in the sky directly before him. Its light shines brightly, sparkling on the waters of the sea. The rest of the dark blue sky is cloudless. The air is still and quite fresh.

This man is robed in the finest, silkiest, colors-of-the-rainbow robe; he is proud of his looks and glances all around at the people in the streets. He is proud of his house; he lives in the finest, biggest house in town. He carries himself like a proud man always does, absolutely sure that everyone else is just as impressed with him as he is with himself. He walks down the street with a long, sure step.

But as he passes the bakery, the baker rushes inside to avoid him.

As he passes the butcher's shop, the butcher does the same.

As he passes the synagogue—the church—its teacher rushes inside.

As he arrives toward the marketplace, all the sellers look away.

You see, no one likes this man—whose name is Matthew—because Matthew is the tax collector for this town. He works for the Roman government, and he likes to lie a little, to steal a little, to get rich on other people's hard work. So that rainbow robe, his fancy sandals, his boat down in the harbor, his house up on the hill—all of it is bought and paid for by lies, by stealing. And the looks on the townspeople's faces—sneering, glaring, frowning, sticking out their tongues behind his back tells you everything you need to know about Matthew's life.

He arrives at his desk in the city center. He sits down and calls over his assistant with a question. As he begins stacking up coins and claims on his desktop and arranges his files, a line is forming before him of taxpayers coming to pay.

Matthew opens his cashbox and smiles at the first person in line. "Next!" he says, loudly.

Now imagine *you* are Matthew, sitting at your desk, looking at all those people waiting in the heat of the day, holding money in their hands that you would like a little of. You are hearing the whispers of the people standing before you:

"What a *scoundrel*..."

"I can't *believe* him..."

"What a terrible, *terrible* person he is!"

"*Next!*" you call.

And just as that person is stepping forward...

Something else catches your eye.

You see a Man who is approaching your desk from the side. He crosses the cobbles of the square, walking rather briskly. He seems to be coming right to the head of the line...

You turn to look.

You wonder what sort of Person might be trying to jump the line.
And that's when you see who He is:

Jesus.

The Teacher.

He is smiling broadly, moving swiftly, His arms hanging loosely at His sides as He, joyfully, strolls along. And, sure enough, He is coming right to where you are sitting. He is coming to the front of the line.

He arrives.

He smiles at you and then leans forward over your desk, plants His fists upon its top, and says, speaking right into your wondering face,

"Matthew, the tax collector! Follow Me!"

The whole line of people gasps!

They are whispering to each other, *"Doesn't Jesus know about Matthew, about tax collectors?"*

"Hasn't He ever heard the way they lie and cheat and steal and make themselves rich by taking what's not theirs?"

And while they are whispering these words, wondering if Jesus has made the most tremendous mistake in the world...

You find you are standing up!

You are looking around at all the money, all the coins, all your important files...

You are thinking about your job, your future, your hopes and dreams...

You are thinking about what your wife and children might say...

You are thinking about your reputation in the village...

And yet, looking into the eyes of Jesus, feeling the love of Jesus, sensing the adventure of what it will mean to follow Jesus...

You go off with Him!

The two of you walk away together, just like that.

This is the true beginning of your whole life.

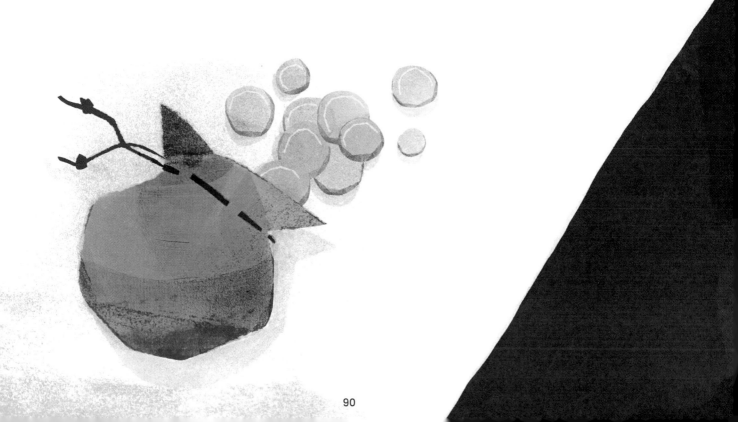

Let's Talk about It

What do you think it would be like to be Matthew? How do you think it would have felt to have all of those people talking about you?

What is it about Jesus that makes people want to leave everything behind to follow Him?

Chapter 8

If Only

Imagine if, for the longest time—for twelve long years of your life—you have been terribly, terribly sick. You have been cut off from friendship because of your sickness. In your day and time, having the type of sickness you have means other people have started to think of you as being "unclean." They would rather walk away than get close to you. They are afraid that being near you will somehow hurt them. So, from the day when you first heard the doctor's words, it's been the same thing almost every single day:

Trying to take care of your illness.

Trying to find someone who cares, who can help.

Yet feeling always worse, all the time.

You've been to countless doctors, up and down the seacoast, and yet they all say the same thing to you as that very first one, "I'm not sure what to do for you."

All of it has been so terribly discouraging.

You feel so sadly confused.

You feel so totally alone.

Desperate.

That is, until earlier today.

You had been sitting on the outskirts of town, under the shade of a tree, when, down by the harbor shore, you started hearing those happy, shouting voices. You listened closely to hear what the townspeople were shouting about. *"He's coming! He's coming!"* you could clearly hear them say.

Standing to your feet, you wandered down through the shadows and hot sunlight toward the place where the market meets the shoreline. The whole town seemed to be pressed into the narrow path next to the market stalls. Men, women, and children were shouting, laughing, calling to each other in the loudest voices. *What's it all about?* you wondered to yourself. You crept a little closer. You were nearly to the edge of the crowd when you started hearing the name of...

Jesus.

"Jesus is coming!" *"Jesus* is on that boat!" "Bring all the sick ones to *Jesus!"* These were the sorts of things the townspeople were shouting. You were standing on the outside of the crowd, watching to see what happened.

Then, sure enough, a steady morning breeze out of the east brought a small fishing boat toward your town's harborline. In the bow of the boat sat a Man smiling at the gathered crowds. The boat beached; out He climbed and was surrounded.

You were edging around the outside of the crowd, trying to get a view of the Man, but you couldn't see what was happening at the center.

Then the whole crowd started moving up, away from the water, and you could only just barely see the Man, Jesus, walking swiftly in the middle. He was pressed from all sides by all these hundreds of people, especially as they walked up through the narrow place by the market. You could see He was walking with the most important man in town.

And that was the moment when the thought first entered your head: *"If only I can just touch His cloak, I'll be healed."*

This idea came to you like a flash of lightning.

"If only I can just touch His cloak, I'll be healed."

You started pressing forward into the noisy crowd. You started winding your way through the press of people.

Now, ever since the doctor had found your sickness, ever since all others had thought you to be "unclean," you had always avoided crowds like this one. You didn't like the looks on people's faces, and the way they jumped aside to avoid you. It was terribly embarrassing to experience, over and over again.

But, right now, you've stopped caring.

You continue moving forward.

"If only I can just touch His cloak, I'll be healed."

Suddenly, there He is. Just ahead of you.

Silently, you hold out your hand. Your fingers extend. You feel the rough cloth of His cloak for just a second...

And the healing comes upon you—spreading like warmth from Him to you. You feel His perfect power flowing up your arm and into your body. It passes upward through your shoulder into your head, heart, belly, down to your legs: *You are healed— instantly!*

Your next breath feels like Heaven—all the weight of twelve long years is suddenly gone as you breathe in and breathe out, *free!*

You start to turn away, a smile spreading across your face...

The people around you haven't even noticed you...

You are now almost to the outside edge of the crowd...

You are so happy you can't believe it...

And then you hear His voice, *"Who touched Me?"*

A shiver runs down your spine. The whole crowd grows quiet. Jesus says again, loudly: *"Who touched Me?"*

One of His friends laughs and says, "Jesus, *everyone* is touching You!"

But Jesus is looking all around the crowd, searching. "I know," He says. "But someone has touched Me, looking for a healing. I have felt the power going from Me to them."

You start to shake with fright.

You are the one He's speaking of.

You are the one He's searching for.

Quickly, you steal a glance in His direction. Your eyes meet. He smiles. He knows.

So you run to Him, falling down at His feet, and you begin to tell the sad, painful story of these twelve long years.

He listens.

He smiles.

He knows.

"My child," He says to you, looking into your eyes like a loving Father, "you have had great faith and your faith has healed you."

You are not quite sure how to respond to these words. He simply smiles at you.

You have never felt seen like He's seeing you now.

In a moment, He is off.

And you decide to follow after Him.

Let's Talk about It

Have you ever felt really sick? What was that like for you?

What do you think made the sick person press through to touch Jesus like that? How do you think she felt when Jesus called her, "My child"?

Chapter 9

Seeing Jesus

Imagine watching a man who wakes in the morning, stretches his arms, reaches out with his toes, yawns big and broad, and then, opening up his eyes—*sees nothing at all.* This man has never seen a single sight in his whole life. To say it another way, the man we are imagining is blind.

Just now, he is preparing to get up and go beg for his daily bread when...

What's that?

What's all that sound?

He rises from his bed and he listens to that noise in the distance. It is the sound of voices echoing his way from the town center. He puts on his robe over his tunic and walks out. All of Bethsaida, his town, seems to be stirring.

The voices grow louder as he, carefully, walks closer. He is almost over to the center of town. That's when he starts hearing one particular Voice speaking clearly, up ahead.

"The Kingdom of Heaven has arrived!" the Voice says, joyously. *"Change your ways! Follow Me!"*

Suddenly, our friend feels the grip of hands around his extended arm. A group of friends start drawing him closer to the Voice.

"Teacher," one of them says. "Can You heal this man? He cannot see at all."

The blind man feels so terribly embarrassed for his friends—*what a request!* Who does he think is able to heal eyes blind since birth?

But the Teacher speaks directly to him, "Alright. Come along. Let's you and I go for a walk together."

The blind man likes the way those words roll off the lips of the Man. There is a steady calm, a humble sort of power, a gentle hint of love in the way those words come forth. He feels an arm across the top of his shoulders. His hand is gently taken by the Teacher's. And now they walk together, moving out and away from the town's center—away from Bethsaida—toward the place where the shore meets the trees.

The Teacher doesn't say a word while they walk that way.

Our friend enjoys the silence and the scent of this kindhearted Stranger.

He is listening to the sounds of the morning breezes, the footsteps of their feet, the tossing of the big palm fronds until...

the Stranger stops.

Then the blind man hears a familiar sound, a sound he didn't expect to hear from the quiet Stranger—the sound of the Man spitting! *"Hock!"* He clears His throat, thickly. *"Pfooo!"* goes the sound of His spit shooting out.

"I am going to touch your eyes," the Voice said to the blind man, kindly. And then...

What's this?! he is thinking to himself. Those hands upon his eyelids are warm, wet and sticky. *Did He just spit on His hands and then touch my eyes with them?!*

"Now open your eyes!" the Voice says, and from the tone of His voice, the blind man knows He is smiling, almost laughing.

So... he does.

He opens his eyes.

Except...

Now he is seeing things!

Where before it was darkness, blackness, emptiness, nothingness, lostness, blindness—now it is *light, colors, fullness, things, experiencing, seeing!* Yes, everything looks a tad bit blurry—the people over there looking like some sort of shapes. But this is all *amazingly exciting, totally overwhelming, absolutely stupendous!*

"Are you seeing anything?" the Voice asks our friend.

Our friend looks to his left to see the face of the Man. He, too, is a tad bit blurry, but just as the blind man expected, He is wearing a great big smile.

"I see some people over there," the blind man says, pointing. "They look a little bit like the trees I sometimes run into."

The Man's face now frowns. "Well, that's not good enough for *Me,*" He says, thinking to Himself.

Then He reaches forth—our friend *sees* His hands coming toward him!
And again He touches the eyes of the man who used to be blind. His big thick thumbs rub against his eyelids; the palms of His hands, the length of His fingers are spread along the sides of his face.

"And what about now?" the Teacher asks.

Our friend opens his eyes again. And now he is looking upon the lovely setting all around himself—the seaside, the seagulls, the tall palm trees. And he is *seeing* now the little waves coming into shore; he is *seeing* the bright daytime colors upon the hillsides. He is *seeing* all the townspeople over there—just down the beach—and he is *seeing* how they react to his sight.

But most importantly, just to his left—there at his side—he is *seeing* the eyes of the Man who wouldn't leave him *half*-seeing. He is *seeing* the smile spreading upon that Man's lips. He is *seeing* the way that this Man loves him.

And now he *can't* see any other way of life than simply going with this Man, following after Him, wherever He might lead.

"Who *are* You?" our friend asks his Healer.

"I am Jesus," He answers. "Now come! Follow Me!"

Let's Talk about It

What do you think the blind man thought when Jesus spat in the dirt?

What would it be like to see for the first time in your life?

What do you think Jesus' smile looks like?

Chapter 10

The Man in the Tree

Imagine sitting at a big desk in an office. It is a beautiful office with a fine polished desk, table and chairs. On the top of your desk are your most prized possessions: an award for your work, a letter from the governor, a statue made of gold. The gold of the statue sparkles with the warm, morning sunlight coming in through the window.

You are sitting at your desk, looking forward to the work of the day. You open one of the desk drawers, looking for something or other. At the back of the drawer, behind your *very* full cashbox, peeking its head out from behind some other papers—you see an old letter you've kept there. You take out the letter and reread it; it is almost three years old.

I am writing to let you know that I'll be ending my work as a tax collector. I am resigning my post, as of today. Thank you for being a good boss to me and to all the others of us in Galilee. I will send the governor a note of gratitude for your leadership.

I am leaving today to follow a Teacher, Jesus from Nazareth in Galilee, who I believe to be the Savior of the world. I believe, in fact, that He may be God and man at the very same time!

He has called me to come and follow along with Him. I must go. I wish you could get a glimpse of the Man—He is everything!

Again, thank you for your help over these last many years.

I am,

Gratefully,

Your friend,

Matthew of Capernaum

You put the letter back in the back of the drawer. You ring your bell for your secretary. "Send in the first person!" you shout.

Your secretary pops his head in through the cracked door. "Sir," he says, quietly, "there is no one come to pay today."

"No one?"

"Not a one, sir," he says. "Word in the street says a crowd is gathering out on Main. Waiting for someone. Some are saying a Teacher of some sort, sir."

"How strange!"

"Indeed, sir."

"And what is this Teacher's name?" you ask.

"Jesus," the secretary says. "Jesus from Nazareth."

Suddenly, you are very, very interested. You glance back down at the letter in your drawer. You look up at your secretary. "I might just go and see for myself," you say.

You rise and put on your bright red overcoat.

You walk back out of your office, down the outside flight of stairs to the street, then around the corner to where your street meets Main Street. Sure enough, a crowd is starting to gather in the morning light. There are mothers and fathers, children out of school, businesspeople, grocers, gardeners, shepherds, beggars—all of Jericho seems to be gathering together!

You stand there, squinting your eyes as you look at the big noisy crowd, and then turn to your right and continue along walking. You wind your way through all the people on this side of the street, doing your best not to have to talk to any of them.

Suddenly you stop. You look around. Your head swivels left and right, looking at all these people around you. You stand up on the tip-tip-top of your tiptoes, straining your neck to see over the top of the crowds, and that's when you realize...

You are too short to see what's happening in the roadway.

Oh, how frustrating!

You begin looking back and forth, back and forth. Is there any break in the crowd? Is there a place where you can slip through to see?

And that's when you notice the sycamore planted along the roadside. Its first growth of branches is just a little higher than your arms can reach. So you take a few steps backward, squaring your shoulders for a charge, and then you rush forward and...

Leap to catch a low branch!

You only barely catch hold—but you just do. Then, awkwardly, you throw a leg over another branch and try to get your whole body up. You reach higher—just getting a hold of the next branch above—and then, like a ladder, start to climb a little more smoothly. Higher and higher, upward, you go and go and go. Your brow is already glistening with sweat.

Finally, you arrive almost to the top of the tree. The branches beneath you shake. Your bright red robe, you imagine, looks funny amidst the green leaves of the tree.

"Here He comes!" voices start to shout. *"Jesus of Nazareth—He is nearly here!"*

A Man—a glorious, bright-smiling, joyful, beaming sort of Man—is walking with great big strides into Jericho. He is followed by His twelve closest friends and, behind them, the crowds of people who seem to always follow Him everywhere. As He nears the spot below your tree, the shouts of the people rise and rise. Then…

Jesus stops.

Right there.

Just below, in the shadow cast by your tree.

The whole crowd quiets down at His sudden, unexpected stop.

Slowly, His smiling face looks upward. His neck leans back as His eyes rise up your sycamore tree. There are lines of laughter spreading from the edges of His eyes. He looks ready to break out into laughter as He shouts loudly upward at you:

"Zacchaeus! I need you to come down immediately—*right now!* I'd like to have lunch at your house."

From your perch in the tree, you don't know what to say. *"Me?!"* you hear yourself asking.

"Of course you!" Jesus shouts up. "Now come on—I want to go to your house!"

So you try to climb down swiftly and neatly, but you have never tried to climb down a tree when your whole town was watching! It suddenly feels very difficult! So, at the second or third branch down, you suddenly tumble—only just barely slowing your fall—and then *bump, bump, bump, bump, bump!* down you come.

You land on the ground right at Jesus' feet. He is standing there and smiling at you. He kneels down and looks you in the eye.

And something begins to happen in your heart...

Something unexplainable...

Something overwhelming...

This most remarkable thing—the most memorable thing you've ever experienced, ever known—comes over you all at once. It seems to come from looking into Jesus' eyes. Great big tears begin falling down your face. "Lord," you say, nearly whispering, "I have been a bad person up till now. I have cheated people, and I've made my fortune by lying. I'm not worthy of You. But, seeing You, meeting You, I'm done with all that now. In fact, here and now I give up all my fortune to the poor."

You can hardly believe the words you're saying!

Jesus has taken your hand in His, and He helps you up to your feet. You begin walking along the road, away from the crowds, the townspeople.

And He looks at you, still smiling, happy to leave behind all others for the pleasure of a meal together with you. And He says to you, simply, gently, lovingly, "Welcome home, My son."

And you suddenly feel like you've come home forever.

Let's Talk about It

Why do you think so many people were gathering to see Jesus? What were they hoping to experience?

What would you want to eat with Jesus if He came over for lunch? What would you want to do with Him?

Why do you think Zacchaeus confessed the bad things he'd done? What do you think he was feeling?

Part III

Jesus' Blood Paid for Everything

Chapter 11

A Witness on the Mount of Olives

Imagine sitting on the edge of a hillside, in the night, seated next to a warm, glowing campfire. The firelight and the full moon light up everything around you. This whole stretch of hillside, the vines down below and the private rich men's gardens up above, are the lifetime work of your old, worn-out, tired hands. You are a gardener here on the Mount of Olives. You are resting after a long, backbreaking day.

After a time, you get up to go get a drink from the brook. The moon is high; it is very bright through the olive branches. You walk slowly, downward, down toward the flowing of the Kidron stream. Beyond are the moonlight-lit walls of Jerusalem. The whole city seems half-asleep, quiet.

You are almost down to the streamside, just above where the vines run north and south, when you see a group coming down the opposite trail, toward you. A Man and a group of men following behind Him. They walk on down the trail, crossing over the Kidron, and then start climbing up. You are only a few feet away, though they haven't seen you. You then watch the Man, the Leader of the group, suddenly stop. He takes one of your own grapevines in hand. Then you listen to the words He speaks to His friends, beautiful words—truly beautiful.

"I am the true vine," He says, *"and my Father is the One who takes care of the garden. Every branch of mine that does not bear fruit He takes in hand, and every branch that does bear fruit He cares for, that it may bear more fruit…"*

You enjoy listening to the way He speaks these words. *This Man understands the work I do*, you think to yourself. And then the Teacher goes on teaching:

"All of you are already clean because of the words that I have been speaking to you, all along. Abide in Me, and I in you," the Teacher says. *"Just as a branch cannot bear fruit on its own, unless it abides in the vine, so neither can you, unless you abide in Me. I am the vine; you are the branches. Anyone who abides in Me and I in him, he is the one who will bear much fruit, for apart from Me you can do nothing at all…"*

The Teacher continues talking to His friends as He walks off. You follow along in the shadows, trying to hear what He says next.

"Now this is My command to you," He says, *"that you love one another just in the ways that I have loved you. Greater love has no one than this, that he should lay down his life for his friends."*

After that, they continue walking up along the hillside. You are just about to turn back toward the stream. But then, glancing upward, you see that the Teacher has stopped right above a crook in the trail, that He has turned around. He is looking at you—*right in the eyes!* The full moonlight is making His whole face shine, grayish-white, and He smiles at you across the distance. Then He and His friends go walking farther up; you see them going in through the gate at the garden called Gethsemane.

You get your drink and go back to your campfire.

You sit there, poking at the glowing logs. Some of the embers crack and pop; sparks rise up. You continue watching up the trail.

Perhaps thirty minutes pass by.

Then you begin to hear noises, but from down below. From down there by the east gate of the city. Loud voices, shouts, the clanging of armor and swords. Then you can see a group of soldiers and their officers coming this way. They each carry a torch; it lights up their coming brightly. They cross the stream—just as the Teacher had done—and begin coming up this way, right along your spot. You watch them climb the trail, and they go right past you. They are serious like a funeral. They go by this spot and continue climbing upward, led by a man at their head. They enter into Gethsemane.

And it is only a few minutes later—such a short space of time—that you see the soldiers coming back down the trail from the garden.

They have bound the hands of that Man, that Teacher.

They have placed Him under arrest, like a criminal.

And when they come upon your spot, when they pass along the path, you are sitting there watching silently by your campfire. And you look to see the look on the Teacher's face. You want to understand the meaning of His arrest by those soldiers...

And that is when you see that He's looking at you...

Looking over to catch your eye...

And, quietly, just above a whisper, right in the midst of all the soldiers, He says to you, "Come and watch. I will do all this for all of you."

You don't know what He means by this.

But you rise from the fire to go and see.

Let's Talk about It

What do you think Jesus meant when He said to "love one another just in the ways that I have loved you"? What do you think that kind of love would look like?

Think of someone who you could show Jesus-like love for today!

Chapter 12

Walking with Jesus to Calvary

Imagine being in the city of Jerusalem during the week of the festival known as Passover. The city is full to the brim with travelers and worshippers. It is noisy and crowded and quite overwhelming. Strange rumors and events have been happening all week. Like the Sunday before when people filled all the streets, looking upward toward the Olive Mount, watching the coming of the Teacher upon the donkey. You had only heard whispers about Him, about Jesus. He was said to be a Teacher and Healer from somewhere in the Galilee.

Then He came riding by you and you saw Him for yourself. The look of love in His face stole your heart.

But then, this Monday, Tuesday, Wednesday, Thursday, all the people kept whispering and wondering; they were wondering what He would do next. And this morning when you woke up, there were already rumors in the streets that He'd been arrested in the night! *Arrested?* Why in the world would they arrest Jesus?

That's what the whole city seemed to be asking.

So, like so many others, you went toward the Temple to find out more. It turned out He'd already been taken to the governor's palace. And then, like so many others, you went over in that direction; you were interested to see for yourself what was going to happen.

It had already happened before you arrived there—*a death sentence!* Jesus of Nazareth *to die on a cross!*

So you walk back out the gate of Pilate's palace, your heart heavy, and you begin walking up the narrow street outside. The street is filled, both sides, with people curious. Up along the street, between them, you climb up. Then a Roman soldier shouts from below, *"Behold the condemned!"* and the whole street around you turns to look back. Then, first out come the other two—common criminals—and they move up along the road, carrying their tall crosses.

And then you see *Him*.

He is coming through the gate, nearly falling under the weight of His cross, and they've made such a mess of Him. His whole body is bloody under the lash of the whip. And they've crowned Him—*but with thorns!* And the people all around you start to gasp, holding their breaths. Here is the Man they'd all been cheering for, just five days earlier! Now He struggles up the roadway, dragging His cross atop His shoulders, to the sound of all their silence.

"Hey, you! You there!" you hear. You look over. One of the soldiers is pointing his finger right at you. *"You! Yes, you!"* he is shouting, pointing. You can't understand what he wants from you.

Drawing his sword, he then points toward Jesus; he wants you to step out of the crowd and help Him with His cross. You are given no time to think. So you go. You step out from the crowd and meet Jesus there in the roadway.

You walk over and get down low beside Him. He moves over, and now you each take a side of the upper beam. Together you begin walking upward, up the hill. You are like a pair of oxen. This is your yoke together.

As you walk amidst the crowds of people, lining both sides of the road, He is quiet nearly the whole way up. You are listening to His short, painful breaths, and you notice the way His blood is pouring off His body. Back behind you, there's the dragging, scraping sound of the tall beam of the cross; ahead of you is Calvary.

Finally, you arrive up there...

And the soldiers at the top yank the cross from your shoulders...

Jesus turns to you and nods, as if to thank you...

And then they nail Him to the cross.

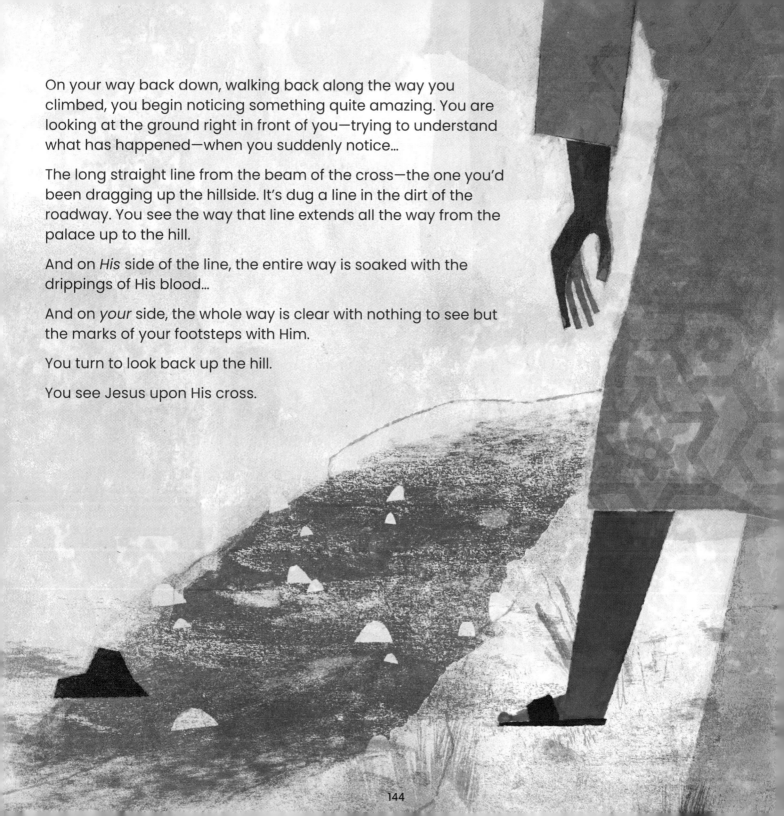

On your way back down, walking back along the way you climbed, you begin noticing something quite amazing. You are looking at the ground right in front of you—trying to understand what has happened—when you suddenly notice...

The long straight line from the beam of the cross—the one you'd been dragging up the hillside. It's dug a line in the dirt of the roadway. You see the way that line extends all the way from the palace up to the hill.

And on *His* side of the line, the entire way is soaked with the drippings of His blood...

And on *your* side, the whole way is clear with nothing to see but the marks of your footsteps with Him.

You turn to look back up the hill.

You see Jesus upon His cross.

Let's Talk about It

How would you have felt to be standing in the crowds when Jesus passed by carrying His cross? How do you think Jesus felt?

What do you think He was thinking about when they nailed Him to the cross?

Chapter 13

The Open Way

Imagine thinking God was far away, hard to know, difficult to please, and that life with Him was a slow, boring, unhappy thing. Imagine thinking that He only lived in one place, that He was only happy with His children when they were living their lives absolutely perfectly. Imagine waking in the morning, feeling fairly certain that He was already angry with you, that all you could do was just to hang your head and feel ashamed of yourself. Imagine falling asleep each night, certain that you'd fallen short and wouldn't be able to do any better tomorrow.

Now imagine being a person whose job, whose whole life, whose absolutely everything was all tied up in the practice of a religion like that. Imagine being a priest, a Levite, in the first century, in the capital city of Jerusalem.

You wake up. You go through your sad, old prayers. You get ready. You have breakfast. Then you put on your fancy robe and priestly clothes. You walk from your house to the *one place in the world* where you believe that God lives.

Today is *your* day.

Today, *you* will be the priest who gets to stand the closest to God in the Holy of Holies—*what a day!*

So now you're going through all your special religious washings—sprinkling this, cleansing that—and putting on a whole other holy, special sets of robes and clothes. And now you're taking a special walk, back toward the gateway, preparing yourself to walk directly forward toward the most special, most holy part of the whole Temple.

You pass swiftly through that first court, through the second gate, past the big altar, where some of your other priest-friends are making sacrifices to cleanse sin. The sight of this action always makes you feel a little sick to your stomach. (You wish in your heart that there was *one* sacrifice to finish them all.)

Then you weave your way past others who are washing their hands in the large bronze laver—a sort of washing bowl for cleansing away the blood. The light of the sun is bright upon its polished rim. (You sometimes wish its fresh, cool waters could cleanse *all* people for *all* time.)

Now it's a straightaway—the crowd of worshippers moving aside as they see you coming—toward the front of the building where the Holy Place stands. You climb up the big, broad steps approaching the golden doors. You feel your heart starting to beat a little bit faster; you are starting to walk more slowly as you approach its entrance.

The golden doors are opened for you, right and left. You cross over the step into the coolness of the Holy Place.

When the servants then close the doors behind you, all is dark, all is hushed; your eyes are trying to see the scene around you. You wait for a moment as your eyesight starts to clear. Your nose is already smelling a thick, strong fragrance.

On your right is a table with twelve pieces of bread upon it; on your left—the only light in the darkness of this big room—is the beautiful golden lampstand with its flames twinkling.

Just ahead is the altar covered up in incense—that's what you've been smelling. Behind that is the great curtain.

The great curtain is the entrance to the Holy of Holies. Only the High Priest ever gets to go in there. The curtain stands high as a tall tree, forty feet upward. Its broad, thick cloth is covered in woven designs. To be honest, you would be afraid to even touch it. You don't feel worthy of His perfect presence.

So, standing where you are, just a few feet away facing the great curtain, you begin to pray the prayers you're supposed to pray, standing in this exact place. One, two, three, four prayers for yourself, then prayers for the priests, then for the people, then for the whole world. You aren't thinking about anything in particular—it is easy enough to pray through prayers you've memorized long before. It is simple to say the things you're supposed to say.

And in this way, a few hours pass by...

In fact, you are almost beginning to come to the end of your special prayers...

You are even starting to think about your evening, the weekend coming up, what you will do, who you will see, when...

What in the world is that?!

What is that loud, ripping-rending sort of sound?!

You open your eyes from your prayers...

You slowly raise your eyes; you look upward...

And you see what is happening right in front of you!

The enormous, broad, thick, woven cloth of the curtain into the Holy of Holies...

is tearing from the top down!

It's like a pair of heavenly hands is reaching downward, grabbing each edge, and—with no effort at all—simply tearing apart the way to God!

Your heart feels like it's stopped beating...

Your knees start to shake...

You can feel the way your face is turning ghostly white...

You turn and run back outside!

You run out the double doors of the Holy Place, out onto the steps...

And outside, where everything is in darkness, like night!

You slowly start to make your way back down the steps toward the laver, toward the altar, toward the courts; but now the sky is beginning to clear overhead. The darkness starts to roll away, like a scroll, and now you can see the shocked faces of the other priests around you.

They are looking away, up to the hillside...

You turn with them to see...

The terrible sight of a Man, on a cross, who has only just hung His head in death...

Though you don't know it yet, you have just witnessed the death ending death and the Life giving His life so that all may enter the Presence of God.

Though you don't know it yet, the evil one is beaten—the Rescuer's rescue is completed for all people, for all time.

The sight of the cross takes your breath away.

Let's Talk about It

What do you like to talk about with God?

Have you ever thought that God was mad at you? Take a moment and ask God, instead, what He thinks about you!

Chapter 14

"But Remember, He Said..."

Imagine sitting on a chair, in the corner of a darkened room, watching all the people around you as they go through all sorts of feelings and emotions. You are a little child. You have been seated on this chair and told to stay put, right there. You are swinging your legs, which are still too short to reach the floor, and you are singing a little song to yourself as you watch all the others.

Some are pacing up and down the room, crying.

Others are actually shaking with fear; their eyes shut.

Some are sitting down on the floor, moaning, sobbing.

A few are so filled with emotion that they seem to be all frozen up inside.

So every once in a while, you get up from your seat, cross the room toward one of these adults and remind them, "But remember, He *said*..."

And every time, that adult will open his eyes or turn her head toward you and remind you that you don't know what you're talking about—*which you most certainly do!*

Three nights ago, Jesus Himself was in this room. He sat at the table—just over there—and ate the Passover supper. Then He took His closest friends up to a garden, somewhere up on the Mount of Olives, and then some bad men came and arrested Him in the dark moonlight. Then some *other* bad men—though they pretended to be good-hearted leaders of God's people—decided that Jesus ought to die for being who He actually is. Then the governor, a Roman man named Pilate, went along with the plan; he somehow decided that it was good for Jesus to die.

All of the friends and followers of Jesus were so upset. It was like they just couldn't believe it. And that was when you started saying, over and over, the same thing. You kept going up to them on that Friday morning, reminding them of all the times He'd already told you about all these happenings happening.

You kept saying to them, "But remember, He *said*..."

And the grownups just kept waving you off.

Then the Roman soldiers beat up Jesus, mocked Him, made Him wear a crown of thorns, and marched Him up the hill to die. They drove the nails through Jesus' hands and feet; then they lofted up the cross and there He hung, looking out over the city. Then the people called Him names, made a joke of all His pain, and all the while, over His head, hung the words of truth: "Jesus, the King." After many hours of struggling, straining, hurting, and hanging there, dying for us, He cried those wonderful words, *"It is finished!"*

All of the friends and followers of Jesus were beside themselves. They just couldn't believe that He was dead, it seemed, and gone.

And you kept saying to them, "But remember, He *said*," and they just kept *shooshing* you, sending you off, seating you on a chair in the corner.

Then a man named Joseph, of the town of Arimathea, came along with a Pharisee, Nicodemus, who'd also once met Jesus. They took His body down from the cross, lovingly wrapped it up in long, winding cloths, and took it to a brand-new tomb, like a cave cut in the hillside. Then they placed His body back there in the dark-black back of the tomb; they said a prayer and then sadly walked back outside. Then the workmen came and—pushing with every ounce of all their strength, all their muscles—rolled a huge rock across the cave's mouth.

All of the friends and followers of Jesus simply wept. That Friday night was the end of the world, they all thought.

But you kept reminding them, coming along beside them, whispering these words into their ears, over and over: "But remember, He *said*..."

And yet no one seemed to listen to you.

And Saturday came.

And then Sunday.

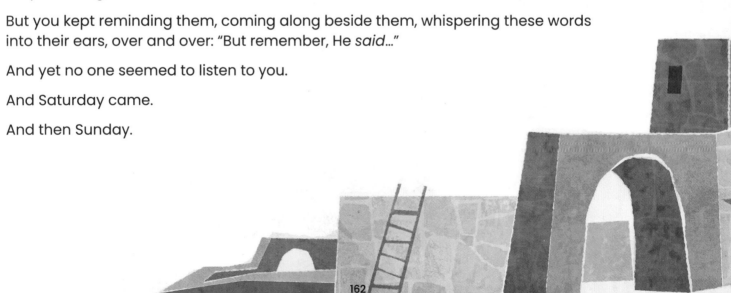

Then away went Mary Magdalene, with some of the other of the best of the ladies, walking toward the tomb in the darkness before the dawn of the day. Then she was suddenly running back into the room and taking Peter and John with her. After seeing the tomb for themselves, Peter and John came wandering back into the room, seeming absolutely and totally confused. Then here came Mary Magdalene again, with the most beautiful smile upon her face, shouting aloud to all, "I've *seen* Him!"

All of the friends and followers of Jesus acted so amazed. The words she spoke to them seemed too marvelous.

And you got up from your seat in the corner, put your arms around the waist of Mary Magdalene, and reminded them, "But remember, He *said*..."

Then, later on, a pair of men who lived in a different town, called Emmaus, set off walking to get back home before suppertime. Everyone else continued waiting in the upper room—doors locked, windows barred—and wondered what the rest of the day might hold. The dark of night was falling when you suddenly heard the sound of running feet coming up the outside stairs. And here came the men of Emmaus, laughing, singing, crying tears of joy, shouting wildly, "He's *alive!* We've seen Him too!"

All of the friends and followers of Jesus just stared at them. They wanted to hear the tale of these strange words.

And from your seat in the corner—just as you were about to say those words for about the *thousandth* time—something far better was happening instead...

Jesus.

Was standing.

Right there!

He was standing in the middle of the room, in the middle of the circle.

He was standing in the middle of all His friends and followers, smiling that wonderful smile of His, and He said, *"Peace be with you!"*

Jesus.

Alive.

With you.

And while the others were all gasping and gaping, screaming and shouting, acting like they'd had no idea this was possible, you felt almost sorry for all those grownups. You wished they'd only just remembered all the times He'd told them. You wished they'd simply believed everything He'd already said.

Jesus crosses the room toward you.

He puts His hand upon your shoulder.

"I bet you kept reminding them, didn't you?" He says.

You nod your head.

"I knew you would," He smiles at you.

"Well," you say to Him, "You *did* say!"

Jesus laughs that wonderful laugh of His.

Let's Talk about It

Why do you think it was hard for people to believe it when Jesus told them He would come back from the dead?

What do you think Jesus looked like when He came into the room where the disciples were praying? Describe it or draw a picture!

Chapter 15

Set Free Forever

Imagine having a terrible secret: a secret so truly terrible that you'd do anything in the whole wide world to *keep* it a secret. You'd be happy to tell a lie, make up stories, run away from everything and everyone if it meant keeping that secret a secret for all time. You'd walk away from friends, pretend nothing really mattered to you anyway, harden your heart until it was hard enough to be something like a wall. You'd be willing to go the rest of your life, never really trusting anything or anyone, just so long as your secret never came back out into the daylight.

Now imagine if that terrible, dark, shameful, painful secret was the fact that you'd actually betrayed your best friend in the whole world, Jesus. You can't stop thinking about what you did on that night.

In fact, you're thinking about it right now.

Yes, you've already seen Him—*ALIVE!*—and, yes, you're still simply amazed that Jesus has already defeated sin and death forever. Yes, you're overjoyed that, on the third day after hearing He was in a tomb, you actually *SAW HIM* standing in the middle of the upper room. These are fantastic, glorious, outstanding facts, too wonderful for words.

And yet...

You can't stop thinking about the three separate times, on that night before the cross, when you told those people you'd never met Him. You can't stop wondering, now that He's risen and returned, whether He knows what you did—*or if someone else has already told Him*. You can't stop listening to every single word He says, listening to His tone of voice, noting the look in His eyes, trying to determine if He's been judging you. You feel you can't quite trust your friends anymore—*Who knows? Who doesn't?* And so you feel so terribly alone with your terrible secret.

Right now, you are sitting, with your elbow upon the bow of your fishing boat, sailing homeward from a night of fishing. You and your friends have caught nothing at all, all night. Everyone is quiet with the feeling of frustration. At your back, the sun is slowly creeping up over the distant hills; the air on the water is cool and feels a little misty. Your friend, John, is handling the sail line and tiller in the stern. You look back at him.

It reminds you again that John, one of your oldest friends in the world, was the only one of the twelve who was also there that night! It gets your stomach all in knots when he looks at you; perhaps he was just that moment thinking of your betrayals of Jesus.

John smiles at you in the sunrise light.

What does that smile mean? you wonder to yourself.

Then, suddenly, you see his eyes light up.

What is John looking at?

You turn toward the shore, and standing there on the beach in the morning's darkness, is a Man. He is standing next to a warm, glowing campfire, just a few feet up from the edge of the water. He raises His hands to cup His mouth and starts shouting out,

"Have you caught anything, boys?"

There is no worse question to ask fishermen who've caught nothing! Together, everyone shouts back, *"No!"*—some with a little hint of anger in their voices.

Then the Man shouts out again,

"Then throw your net on the OTHER side of the boat!"

What an incredibly strange idea! This boat, after all, is only about ten feet wide at its widest point. And you've been fishing *all night* and *all night* you've caught nothing—not a fish, not a guppy, nothing at all.

And yet...

You and your friends are all looking around at each other.

There is something so familiar about that Stranger on shore.

And so now you're standing up together, unfolding the carefully folded-up net as a team, and now—*SPLASH*—away it goes...

Down, down, down, down, down it sinks...

And together you begin pulling at the line to draw the weights together...

Then, OH!

The net is so heavy.

So full of colorful, big, fat, flopping fish.

Suddenly, you *know!*

But your friend, John, has already beaten you to the punch. He points at the Man on the beach, "That's the Lord! That's Jesus!"

And, despite your terrible secret, despite the feelings you were feeling only moments ago, you are already diving off the front of the boat!

Despite your terrible secret, He's still your best friend.

Despite the secret, He's still Jesus.

After the others arrive, dragging in the net so full of fish, you all then sit with Jesus over the most marvelous, simple, yet delicious breakfast. The low glowing of the fire warms you up—wet as you are from your swim in—and you all sit in a circle, enjoying His presence.

After eating, He looks at you. "Shall we take a walk?" He asks.

"Just us?" you ask back.

"Just you and Me," He says.

He rises to His feet, extends a hand toward you, and you rise and begin your walk together. You are feeling suddenly terribly nervous with Him. Perhaps *this* will be the moment of your punishment. Perhaps He will walk you down the beach, talk about your three-times betrayal, and then say, "This is where we'll say goodbye."

You are listening to the crunch of your sandals on the pebbly shore.

You are still somewhat damp, with a shiver going up your spine, when you feel His arm going around your shoulder...

"Let me ask you, do you *love* Me?"

You couldn't be quicker with your immediate answer, *"Oh yes, Lord!"*

He looks over at you as you look over at Him, and He says, quietly, kindly, "Then feed My sheep, will you? Love others as you have seen Me love."

You walk along for another minute or two in silence...

"Here's a question," He says to you, breaking that silence, "do you love *Me?*"

Again, you couldn't be quicker with your response, *"Yes, Lord!"*

He looks at you as you're looking over at Him, and He says, quietly, kindly, "Then lead My sheep, will you? Lead everyone to Me as I've led all people to My Father."

You continue walking on...

Perhaps five minutes pass...

The shore of the lake is curving up ahead...

"How about this," He says, "and I want to hear your truest, most honest response from the bottom of your heart, *do* you love Me?"

You stop and turn to face Him. Jesus turns and faces you. The two of you stand there, looking at each other. You are feeling somewhat hurt by these three questions. After all, you would've thought that Jesus, already knowing everything about everything, would've already known the way you love Him, the way you've *always* loved Him— *always!*

"Yes, Lord!" you say, quite intently. "You know *all* things, and You *know* that I love You!"

Jesus is smiling broadly.

"Then will you feed My followers for Me?" He asks. "Will you be the one who follows My Way, no matter what?"

And you are just about to answer Him...

You are just about to point out John, who's been following...

You are just about to speak up...

When a look flashes over the eyes of Jesus—*you'll never forget it*—and that look speaks louder than words:

"I know your secret—*and I love you still.*"

Let's Talk about It

Have you ever felt regret about something you did to someone you loved? What did that feel like?

Why do you think Jesus didn't punish Peter?

What do you think Jesus meant when He said, "Feed my sheep"?

Part IV

Nothing Is Impossible

Chapter 16

His Return
to Where This All Started

Imagine Jesus having an outdoor meal with His friends. They are sitting on a big circle of comfortable blankets on the Mount of Olives. They are all enjoying their afternoon together. The countryside around them is warm in the bright sunlight. The birds in the trees are singing, happy, and joyful sounding. The disciples and Jesus are just finishing their meal; all feel relaxed. What an absolutely splendid afternoon!

From the place they sit, they are looking down over Jerusalem, over the Temple, over the houses, shops, restaurants, all the way out to where Jesus died. Nearby in the shadows of the tall trees, they can even see the place where His body was once laid inside the tomb.

And yet *here He is,* sitting on the picnic blanket right beside them, finishing a sandwich in the warm sunlight. *It's simply too amazing!*

And speaking of something too amazing...

You won't believe what happens next!

You see, right after He'd been telling them some important things about their future, the disciples suddenly start to see Jesus rising up from the picnic blanket. But not just rising to His feet—*oh no!* It's like, all at once, a pair of heavenly hands are reaching downward and taking Him upward; He just starts rising up, moving swiftly up into the sky! They are all on their feet, with their hands extended—like worshippers—and their eyes are wide and watching as He gets higher, higher, higher.

The loving eyes of Jesus are upon them as He rises...

And then...

He is gone.

He is hidden behind the big, beautiful clouds.

He is returning to where all of this started.

That Place is perfectly, totally silent now. All the angels and saints are holding their breaths. The gleaming golden walls are trembling with the perfect stillness. The Holy Spirit is in the air all around them.

The Throne room of Heaven is waiting. They've all been waiting, for more than thirty years in "earth time," and they can't wait for the moment to arrive. Everyone's eyes are upon those great doors of the Throne room. They are waiting for the arrival of Jesus.

The *Father* is waiting for the arrival of His Son.

Finally, the moment arrives!

Those great, gorgeous golden doors swing on their hinges; a pair of mighty warrior angels open them wide for the entry of the King of kings.

Jesus walks back in...

All of Heaven bows low...

His eyes are looking unto the eyes of His heavenly Father.

And now He walks the center aisle, between angels and saints with tears in their lowered eyes, toward that throne from which He'd once left. He will be taking back His place, the place He'd left to enter the world. All of Heaven is holding its breath for that glorious moment.

He arrives at the steps before the throne...

He is smiling as He looks up at His Father...

And then He climbs those golden steps, His head held high, His footsteps sure, and now He turns to face the gathering of the great Throne room. The angels and saints are watching Him silently. The beaming smile has never left His face.

And Jesus sits down.

All of Heaven explodes in singing, shouting, clapping, cheering, and worshipping as Jesus retakes His seat upon the throne. The angels and saints rejoice to see the King of Kings and the Lord of Lords returning to where this all started. This is the sound of final victory, and the glorious wonder of His words, *"It is finished!"* still rings out over the whole world. It is the song in the hearts of every man, woman, and child who know Jesus, the Christ, the Savior of the world, the Ascended One.

Jesus, upon His throne, turns toward His Father.

The Father smiles at Him and says, "Well done, My Son!"

And Jesus, smiling back at Him, smiling at all the angels and saints, smiling down on His first disciples—*smiling ever upon us!*— says with that wonderful, booming voice of His, with that twinkling of heavenly love in His eyes,

"Now, nothing will be impossible!"

Let's Talk about It

What do you think heaven sounded like when Jesus returned? Why was heaven so happy?

What kinds of things are now possible because of Jesus? Make a list of anything you can think of!

Chapter 17

To the Ends of the Earth

Imagine listening in on a conversation between the friends of Jesus. They are talking together in the stillness of that same upper room. (This is the room where you ate the Last Supper with Jesus—where He washed everyone's dirty feet. It's the very same room where He returned—*and so surprised you!*—after He'd risen again.) You are listening to Peter, James, John, Andrew, and some of the others, and these are the sorts of things they are saying to each other:

"So when do you think He'll return?" someone asks.

"I don't know," another responds. "But the angels said it would be glorious, just like His going-up was."

"And where do you think we should start?" someone else pipes in.

"Start?" others ask. "Start on what?"

"On the mission He gave us to do. Don't you remember what He said to us beforehand? He said, *'You will be My witnesses'*—remember that?— *'My witnesses to Jerusalem, to Judea, to Samaria, and to the very ends of the earth!'*"

"The ends of the earth—that sounds *far*," somebody says quietly.

"It almost seems—*Impossible*," you hear somebody else.

Finally, you speak up, "But don't forget what He said *before* that!"

Everyone's eyes turn to look at you.

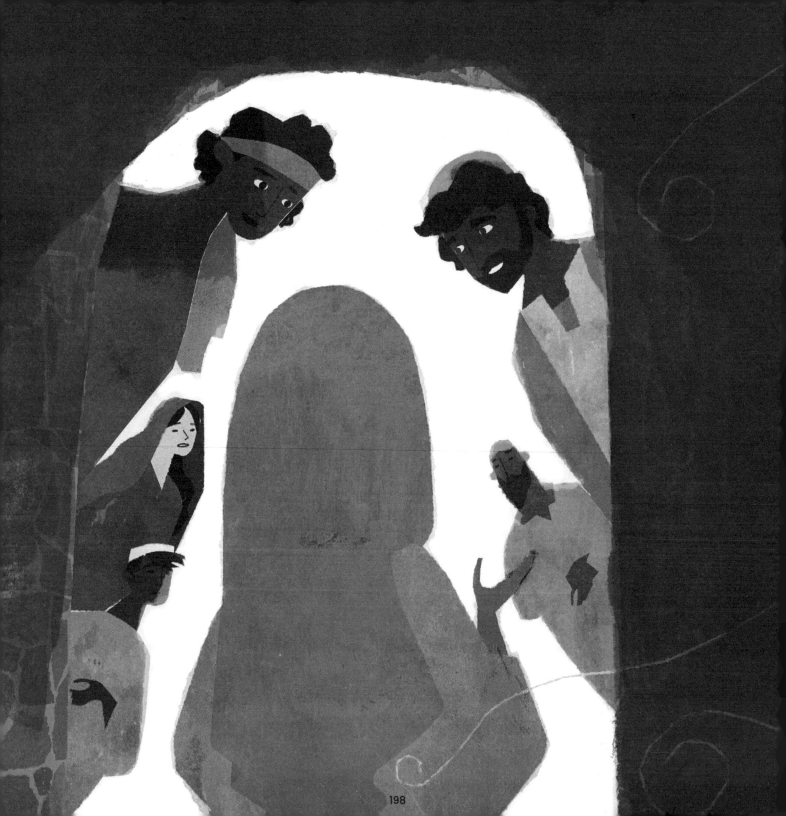

You are standing near the doorway of the upper room; you have been leaning against the wall, listening to the words of this whole conversation. Every face in the room is now turned toward you. They are waiting upon your reminder of the words Jesus spoke just before He ascended back to Heaven.

"What He said," you say, "is, *'Don't leave Jerusalem! Wait upon the Father's gift! You will receive power when the Holy Spirit comes upon you!'* Then He said those other things about places we should go. But don't you remember His words about the Holy Spirit?"

Everyone in the room is nodding along, remembering.

Then someone—it may have been Peter, James, John, or Andrew—asks you this question, "So what do you think we should do *now*?"

"I think we should talk to *Jesus* about it," you reply confidently. "Let's just have a conversation with *Him*."

The whole group—all the friends, followers, disciples and apostles there in the upper room—agrees with your idea for the morning. Everyone waits for you to start the conversation—the conversation with the Lord Jesus Himself.

With a great smile on your face, you begin to pray...

And, almost immediately, *the room starts to fill with a heavenly wind!*

A golden, glowing burning like some mighty, powerful flame hovers above you!

Now at the very same moment, just outside the house where you are gathering, are thousands of people in one of the great squares of Jerusalem. All the houses, shops, and restaurants surround this big open area, and this square is totally full, wall to wall. It is filled by men, women, and children—people from all around the world—who have come to celebrate Pentecost, a special festival. People are trying to buy their breakfasts, others are arguing with sellers in the marketplace—it is a loud, confusing scene out there in the great square. It hardly seems like a place where something holy would happen—but something holy is *definitely happening!*

Because, suddenly, you and the others burst forth from the upper room onto the balcony outside.

You are singing, shouting, speaking wildly, excitedly, loudly of one name—*Jesus!*—and you are speaking of Him in languages you've never known before!

You are standing just to the side of Peter, James, John, Andrew, and the others; your heart is bursting with the joy of being filled with the Holy Spirit of Jesus. The fresh air of the morning, the look of the crowds of people below the balcony, the joy of the Lord, all fill your mouth with singing and the Good News of Jesus.

You are hearing your friends speaking in those foreign languages.

You are wondering what is the meaning of all this newness.

And then you hear the voices of the crowd below. These curious people are looking up toward you and shouting to each other:

"What has happened to these men, women, and children?"

"And how did they learn to speak in all these different tongues and languages?"

"It's like they've studied at the farthest corners of this earth!"

You, Peter, James, John, Andrew, and all the others smile at each other when you hear those last words from the crowd...

Just a few minutes ago, you were wondering about Jesus' plan for reaching the world...

You had felt so small and unimportant, so alone, unseen...

But now with His Holy Spirit within you, with His name upon your lips, with His love burning within your hearts...

Nothing is impossible.

Let's Talk about It

Have you ever tried to say words in a different language? What was that like?

If you could speak any language you wanted, what would you say to people?

Chapter 18

A Curious Walk

Imagine taking an afternoon stroll with your best friend. It is the middle of the afternoon in Jerusalem. You are just walking along, having a pleasant conversation about the things you are noticing along the way.

You are nearly to the gate of the Temple.

Suddenly, your friend, Peter, has stopped short. He is looking very serious about something. He takes a few steps backward, back to where you'd just passed. He crouches down and says to the man sitting there, "What did you say?"

The man, a beggar, repeats his words, "I asked if you might give me something, sir."

"What would you ask that we give you?" Peter asks.

"A coin or two," the man says. "Whatever you've got. Silver or gold—it doesn't matter which."

Peter is looking very intently at the man. "Did I just see that someone carried you to this spot?" he asks.

"Yes, sir," the man replies. "I am not able to walk, you see. Never have. So I beg each day. That's what I do here all day long."

Peter stands swiftly up to his feet beside you. You are standing there in the busy street, looking down at the man. He is beginning to look to other people who are passing by. Then Peter says to him, *"Look at us!"* quite loudly.

The man holds up his begging bowl—with just a few coins in it—and he is clearly expecting that you will throw in another one or two.

Peter clears his throat. He stands up very straight. "Silver and gold, we do not have," he says to the man. "But what we *do* have—what has been given to us forever by the goodness of the Lord Jesus—I'd be happy to give you right now, right here. In the name of Jesus, *walk!*"

You can tell the man is not sure what to say or to do. He is looking up into your eyes with a question upon his face.

Without giving him a second more to think about his questions...

Not waiting even an instant to let the words lose their power...

Peter reaches down and grabs the man by the hand, lifts him up to his feet...

And the man stands!

The man who couldn't walk is now standing...

And trying to walk around...

And then, quite funny to see, trying to hop...

And, even better yet, begins jogging.

The joy in His eyes is the living joy of Jesus.

All the people in the streets, so used to seeing this man sitting there by the gutter, are now moving closer, wanting to understand what has happened. You and Peter continue your walk toward the Temple.

But then, looking back, you realize that the man is following you, and the curious crowds are following behind him, watching everything he does. You realize that it won't be very quiet, or very peaceful, when you arrive at your usual spot in the Temple.

You and Peter stop under the shadow of an archway. This is a place you often come to talk with Jesus. He Himself once stood under this archway, teaching the great crowds; it makes you feel especially close to Him when you return to this spot.

The people are crowding all around you now. The man who couldn't walk is now running around in circles.

A voice in the crowds shouts the question at you, *"What's this all about?"*

And Peter answers, *"Jesus!"*

"Tell us what you mean by that!" the voice shouts.

And Peter smiles and says, *"Happily…"*

Let's Talk about It

What did Peter give to the man that was better than silver or gold?

What would you tell people about Jesus if they asked you?

Have you ever seen a miracle healing? Tell about it! If you could choose, what would you want to see healed?

Chapter 19

The Resurrection and the Life

Imagine following close behind a group of people who are crying, who are sobbing, who are groaning with a deep sadness. You are following them across a quiet square, in the middle of a small town; you are drawing near to the house of one of their friends. The front door opens. Inside are other friends who are also crying, also sobbing, also groaning with the same deep sadness. You enter the house, going through the kitchen, through a back room, and then up a narrow flight of stairs to an upstairs room.

Someone along the way has handed you a candle. You carry it carefully. Its golden light gently flickers within the dark stairway.

You are almost up to the top step...

Your guide takes a deep breath before opening up the door.

Together, you cross across the threshold into the room; the golden candlelight is the only light in its darkness.

And there—on the other side of the room lying on a small bed looking really quite peaceful—is the reason you've been brought to this house this evening. You are looking at the perfectly quiet, perfectly restful face of one of the best friends of all those people who are crying downstairs. This woman's name is Tabitha.

She died earlier this evening.

In the silence of the room, with the flickering light of your candle the only light, you kneel down beside the bed and look at Tabitha's face. She is a beautiful older woman; someone has tucked a lovely lily in her folded hands. All is at peace, quiet. And you are just about to begin praying, just about to ask the Lord for what to do next, just about to seek His face for a wondrous miracle...

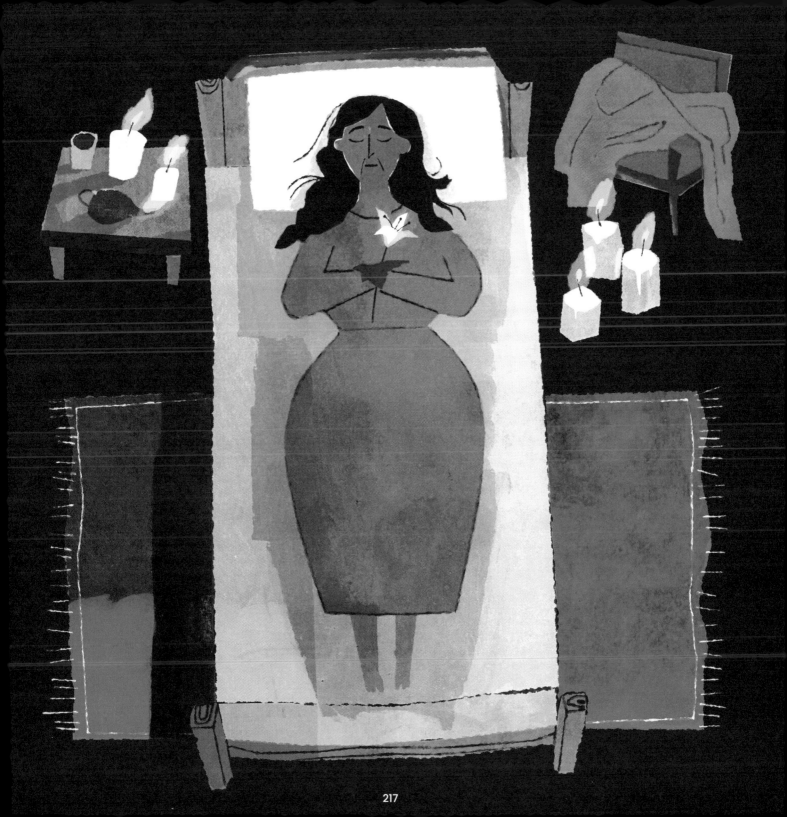

When all of a sudden you are remembering a certain moment—a moment perfectly unforgettable—with your beloved Lord Jesus:

> He was standing at the outskirts of the town of Bethany, near Jerusalem. Martha, the sister of His dear friend Lazarus, was before Him. "Lord," she said, "if only you had been here, I know my brother wouldn't have died!"

> Jesus' eyes grew narrower at those words. "I promise you, your brother will rise again," He whispered.

> Martha continued crying quietly. "I know," she whispered back. "For I believe that he will one day rise again at the Resurrection—that day at the end of all days."

> Jesus stepped forward, toward her. He took Martha by the shoulders. She looks up at Him. His eyes were lit with power and with love in that moment. And He said to her, "Martha, I am the Resurrection and the Life."

> And, minutes later, Lazarus was alive again.

You blink your eyes and look again at the face of the woman before you. You close your eyes and begin praying.

"Lord Jesus," you say, "I am grateful to be Yours; I am grateful to remember the day when You called me to Yourself. I am thankful for the everyday experience of following along beside You, of the words and works I have seen You do. And I know, even right now, just as You used to listen to me on the roads and paths of the Galilee, You are still listening to me. You have never been away from me, Jesus, and I'm so glad You're in this room, and in my heart, and sitting on the throne of Heaven, all at the same time."

A great, broad smile is on your face as you pray these words.

"Now, Lord, seeing as You're the Resurrection and the Life—the Way, the Truth, the Life—I'm coming to ask You for a miracle tonight. Would You reach out Your hand through my life and raise this woman from the dead? Would You do like You did with Lazarus that day? Would You resurrect this dear, good woman, just like the Father raised You?

"For I believe, O Lord, that nothing is impossible anymore.

"I believe that You can do this, right now!"

You open up your eyes, look at the face of the woman lying upon the bed, and then you say to her:

"Tabitha, in the name of Jesus of Nazareth, *get up!*"

What do you think
happens next?

Let's Talk about It

If even death is not too much for Jesus to overcome, is there anything He cannot do?

If He lives inside of us, is there anything we cannot do with Him?

Chapter 20

Even Greater Things

Imagine if you'd *never* seen Jesus, *never* heard the sound of His voice, *never* watched a single one of His miracles, *never* experienced His presence, *never* been anywhere near where He ever was. Everything you know is by hearing it from other people. Yes, you've *heard* of the light in His eyes, the wonderful way He spoke, the amazing things He did, how it felt to be around Him, and you certainly *feel* like you missed out, not meeting Him!

But at least you've gotten to know His friends, the disciples. These are the men and women who once walked with Him along the shores of the Galilee. There is a sparkling light in *their* eyes, there is *passion* in the way they speak of Him, and there are miracles happening in and around their lives *all the time!* You're slowly starting to realize that by being around the friends of Jesus—walking with them, talking with them, asking them questions—it's almost the same as being with Him. His life just seems to keep on going through them.

Take this very afternoon, for instance.

You and a few hundred other people were all standing in a big semicircle, listening to the disciples; you were standing in a part of the Temple called Solomon's Porch. The tall walls of the Temple were high above your head, bright white. The afternoon was warm and comfortable, the wind, quiet. The crowd around you was all leaning forward, listening closely—they didn't want to miss a word about all the glories of Jesus. The final speaker, Peter, finished with what he was saying and began walking off.

"Excuse me," you heard yourself saying to him. "May I ask you a question?"

Peter turns to you and smiles. "Absolutely!" he says. "But I happen to be on my way somewhere. Would you want to talk while we walk?"

You begin walking alongside Peter—out through the outer court, out through the gateway, out into the crowded streets of a busy Jerusalem afternoon. You find that Peter is quite a quick walker; you are almost running to stay beside him. The two of you are weaving in and out of the crowds in the streets.

"So what would you like to ask me?" Peter asks you.

"I'd like to know your top three favorite moments with Jesus," you announce.

Peter lets out a joyful laugh. "Oh, that's impossible!" he says. "How could I only speak of three? There's just too many amazing moments to choose from."

You were somewhat expecting that he might say something like this. "Alright," you say, "then can you tell me just one memory that's been on your mind lately? I'd like to hear the moment that's most important to you, right now."

You are just turning the corner into an even busier street. As you do, Peter's eyes light up. "It was almost just like this!" he says, pointing ahead. "We were walking along a street like this, totally packed with people, and the Lord suddenly stopped and said, *'Who touched Me?'* You see, a woman in the crowd had been having an incredible thought, *'If I can only touch His cloak, I will be healed'* and she'd touched His cloak and been healed!"

He continues walking along, thinking his thoughts to himself.

A minute or two pass by.

"But it was the funniest thing," he says, all at once, almost startling you, "that lady started to tell everyone about what happened to her. Her story spread like wildfire, practically everywhere. And now, everywhere we went, from the biggest city to the smallest town to the tiniest little village, everyone's hands shot forth toward Him. Everyone was sure that simply touching the edge of His cloak—just like that woman— would get the job done, that they'd be healed of anything.

"And, let's be honest, they were right to think so. It was true. The healing power of Jesus was so complete."

You have passed beyond the busy central streets of Jerusalem; the narrow alley you're walking now is quieter. Once again, Peter's voice has trailed off. It is clear he is thinking to himself of how it was to be with Jesus.

A quiet minute or two passes.

"Which always makes me think…" Peter says, then goes silent.

You take another few steps, waiting for him to continue speaking. He is looking ahead at a large group of beggars lying there in the hot sunlight. It is clear that none of them can walk. Peter looks intently up toward them.

"It makes me think of the night before He went to the cross," he goes on, "and of something He said to all our twelve, there in the upper room. He said to us, 'I tell you the truth, anyone who believes in Me will do the *exact same things* as you have seen Me doing.' Isn't that an absolutely amazing promise? And then He went further, 'And I tell you, you will do *even greater things* than these, because I'm going back to My Father.' I think about those words all the time."

You are now drawing near to that large group of beggars along the roadway. Some of them hold up their begging bowls for money.

"And I wonder," Peter is saying to you, "whether that 'even greater things' promise is possible. How could I do *even greater things* than Jesus?"

You are passing the beggars on your left. Peter seems lost in his thoughts. The sunlight is bright in your eyes.

"And yet I just keep waking up," Peter says to you, "starting my day by spending time with Him, being filled up with His presence. And I just keep trying to follow His Way, to love as He loved, to spend my days listening only to His Spirit."

Suddenly, a movement has caught your eye...

You glance back over your shoulder...

You are watching the shadow of Simon Peter, one of the best friends of Jesus,
slowly passing over the beggars...

And then you see the way the looks on their faces change...

How they suddenly look around at each other...

And then rise to their feet!

"Anyhow," Peter is still talking to you, not noticing anything about the miracles happening behind him, "that's the memory I've been thinking about lately."

He looks over at you.

"And what have *you* been thinking about Jesus?" he asks.

You are simply too amazed to answer.

Let's Talk about It

What were some of your favorite moments with Jesus from this book?

What do you think it means for you to do even greater things than Jesus? What kinds of things would He be excited to see you do?

About Bill Johnson

Bill Johnson is the Senior Leader of Bethel Church, Redding. Bethel serves a growing number of churches that have partnered for revival. This apostolic network has crossed denominational lines in building relationships that enable church leaders to walk in both purity and power. Bill is a fifth-generation pastor with a rich heritage in the Holy Spirit, and his priority in life has been to learn how to host the presence of God and minister to Him.

About Eugene Luning

Eugene Luning directs The Union, a ministry within the New Horizons Foundation, which exists for teaching, retreats, podcasting, and spiritual counseling in Colorado and around the country. Additionally, he is the cofounder of a real estate technology company, Panoramiq Markets Inc.

Eugene and his wife, Jenny, are the parents of three children, Hadley, Tripp, and Hoyt. They live in Colorado Springs, Colorado, where they also lead a weekly fellowship, The Anchor.

About Kevin & Kristen Howdeshell

Kevin & Kristen Howdeshell are a husband and wife team illustrating a variety of projects including bestselling children's books, food packaging, movie posters, music albums, and editorial spots. Their work is characterized with texture, a mid-century influence, and a lean toward meaningful family time. They lead up The Brave Union Studio in Kansas City, Missouri, where they raise their three young kids and enjoy their Betta fish, their treehouse, and trampoline. In their non-art hours, Kevin enjoys fly fishing, Kristen likes working in the yard while listening to a baseball game, and both enjoy playing board games with the kids. Follow their work @TheBraveUnion on Instagram.

About the Moments with Jesus Project

The Moments with Jesus Project is committed to helping children and adults encounter Jesus for themselves by engaging Scripture through the power of imagination.

To this end, we offer resources including books, podcasts, videos, and more.

Learn more by visiting our website:
www.momentswithjesusproject.com

Or connect with us on social media:
@momentswithjesusproject

Bethel

We are a community of believers passionate
about God's manifest presence.

We believe that God is good and
our great privilege is to know and experience Him.

To learn more about church, music, events,
media, schools, and more, visit us at:

www.bethel.com

the BILL JOHNSON collection

Bill Johnson

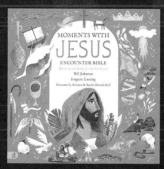

Moments with Jesus Encounter Bible

The King's Way of Life

God is Really Good

Open Heavens

Mornings and Evenings in His Presence

The Way of Life

God is Good

When Heaven Invades Earth

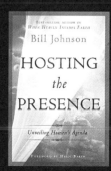

Hosting the Presence

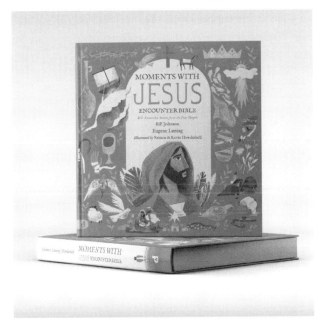